Major John Richardson's

A CANADIAN CAMPAIGN

WITH HIS
RECOLLECTIONS OF THE WEST INDIES

AND

DAVID BEASLEY'S

IN SEARCH OF RICHARDSON'S SPAIN

To Hugh Brown
Best wishes
David Beasley

DAVUS PUBLISHING

SIMCOE, ONTARIO

Library and Archives Canada Cataloguing in Publication

Richardson, John, 1796-1852
Major John Richardson's A Canadian campaign : with his Recollections of the West Indies ; and, David Beasley's In search of Richardson's Spain.

ISBN 978-0-915317-36-3

1. Richardson, John, 1796-1852. 2. Canada--History--War of 1812--Personal narratives. 3. Canada--History--War of 1812--Campaigns. I. Beasley, David, 1931- II. Title. III. Title: Canadian campaign.

FC443.R53A3 2011 971.03'4092 C2011-900406-2

DAVUS PUBLISHING
150 NORFOLK ST S
SIMCOE, ON N3Y 2W2
CANADA
WEB SITE: www.davuspublishing.com
email: davus@kwic.com

CONTENTS

INTRODUCTION by David R. Beasley, Simcoe, ON

"A Canadian Campaign" serialized in the NEW MONTHLY MAGAZINE AND LITERARY JOURNAL [London: Colburn] in 1826 and 1827 became the basis for Richardson's "Operations of the Right Division of the Army of Upper Canada, During the American War of 1812", which he printed in part with documents in his *New Era* [Brockville] newspaper in 1842 and reprinted this newspaper version in book form as WAR OF 1812.

Richardson changed slightly the wording of some paragraphs when transcribing from the essay to the book, *War of 1812*, which Alexander Clark Casselman republished in 1902 as *Richardson's War of 1812 with Notes and a Life of the Author*. Richardson added information to his edition such as personal descriptions of Indian warriors and officers of both armies, and Casselman's edition is replete with informative footnotes. One section from the book, however, I will include herewith—that is Richardson's description of the death of Tecumseh. In my biography of Richardson, *The Canadian Don Quixote*, I mention that Richardson believed that Colonel R. M. Johnson, later U.S. Vice-president, killed Tecumseh, but that later writers suggested others as his killer. Richardson wrote that Tecumseh's body was skinned by American soldiers [for souvenirs or to make razor strops, as reported at the time], Richardson includes in his "A Trip to Walpole Island and Port Sarnia in the Year of 1848"[1] a letter from Shah-wah-wan-noo who said that he saw an American kill the wounded Tecumseh with an axe and cut a piece out of his thigh to show his superiors. Whether Tecumseh was skinned has been a matter of contention, even recently to a reviewer of my creative non-fiction *From Bloody Beginnings: Richard Beasley's Upper Canada,* in which I gave it the space of a half-sentence. Here is Richardson's description from his *War of 1812*.

---

[1] IN *John Richardson Short Stories*, ed. David Beasley (Penticton; Theytus, 1985)

Only a few minutes before the clang of the American bugles was heard ringing through the forest, and inspiriting to action, the haughty Chieftain had passed along our line, pleased with the manner in which his left was supported, and seemingly sanguine of success. He was dressed in his usual deer skin dress, which admirably displayed his light yet sinewy figure, and in his handkerchief, rolled as a turban over his brow, was placed a handsome white ostrich feather, which had been given to him by a near relation of the writer of this narrative, and on which he was ever fond of decorating himself, either for the Hall of Council or the battlefield. He pressed the hand of each officer as he passed, made some remark in Shawnee, appropriate to the occasion, which was sufficiently understood by the expressive signs accompanying them, and then passed away forever from our view.

Towards the close of the engagement, he had been personally opposed to Colonel Johnson, commanding the American mounted riflemen, and having severely wounded that officer with a ball from his rifle, was in the act of springing upon him with his tomahawk, when his adversary drew a pistol from his belt and shot him. It has since been denied by the Americans that the hero met his death from the hand of Colonel Johnson. Such was the statement on the day of the action, nor was it ever contradicted at that period. There is every reason to infer then that the merit (if any merit could attach to the destruction of all that was noble and generous in savage life), of having killed Tecumseh, rests with Colonel Johnson. The merit of having flayed the body of the fallen brave, and made razor strops of his skin, rests with his immediate followers. This too has been denied, but denial is vain. On the night of the engagement, when seated around a fire kindled in the forest, partaking, on the very battle ground, of the meat which Gen. Harrison's aids-de-camp were considerately and hospitably toasting for us on long pointed sticks, or skewers, and which, half-famished as we were, we greedily ate without the accompaniment of either salt or bread, the painful subject was discussed, and it is not less an eulogy to the memory of the high-minded Tecumseh, than a justice to that of General Harrison to add, that that officer was the first to deplore his death: while the sentiments he expressed, when the circumstance and manner of his fall were made known, were such as to reflect credit on himself, both as a man, a Christian, and a soldier.

Doubts as to the fact of Tecumseh having fallen at all at the Moraviantown, have, in the same spirit of party which has denied to Colonel Johnson the act of having shot him, been entertained; and it has even been asserted that the mutilated remains which were supposed to have been his, were in reality those of another Chief. Would for the honor of humanity it had been so: but this is incorrect. Several of the officers of the 41st, on being apprized of his fall, went, accompanied by some of General Harrison's Staff, to visit the spot where Tecumseh lay, and there they identified (for they knew well) in the mangled corpse before them, all that remained of the late powerful and intelligent chieftain. Of the pain with which the sight was viewed, and the deep regret with which his death was regarded, no stronger evidence can be given than in the fact that there was scarcely an officer of the captured Division who, as he reposed his head upon the rude log, affording him the only pillow that night, did not wholly lose sight of his own unfortunate position in the more lively emotion produced by the untimely fate of the lamented and noble Indian. It has ever been a source of profound regret to me that I was not present at this inspection, for although the sight of the mutilated hero could not have failed to inflict upon my heart pain of the most poignant kind, it would have been at least a consolation to have seen the last of his remains on earth: and this not more from the reverence and honor in which I had, and have, ever held the Warrior, than from the opportunity I should now possess of bearing attestation to the fact and manner of his fall, from my

> own positive and personal observation. I was not, however, aware of the purposed visit until the party had returned, and made it the subject of conversation, in the presence of General Harrison, as already stated. Nor was there time afforded for remedying the unintentional omission.

Another quotation from Richardson's *War of 1812* refers to his meeting General Harrison thirty-seven years later. Harrison was campaigning at the time for President of the U.S.

> It is a circumstance perhaps not unworthy of remark here that in 1840, after a lapse of twenty-seven years (during three and twenty of which I had been absent from the country), I alone of the force engaged at the siege of Fort Meigs, should have met with General Harrison on the very spot which he so vigorously defended against us in l8l3; and, yet more remarkable, that the occasion of such meeting should have been the commemoration of the events of that important period. It was during the great delegation, or convention, which preceded the gallant old General's elevation to the Presidential chair, and when introduced to him by the Governor of Michigan, as one who had borne arms against him during that siege, and had later become his prisoner, I was received in that spirit of true and generous courtesy which is ever characteristic of the soldier.

Richardson in his EIGHT YEARS IN CANADA [1847] expanded colorfully upon the occasion of this meeting which was at a re-enactment of the Battle of Fort Meigs, still commemorated to this day. In the same book, he described coming upon the scene of the Battle of the Thames in 1840 [pages 129-132]. He was driving a carriage from Montreal to Windsor and had just suffered an accident. His account adds interesting details and reveals his sarcasm for his general, Procter, who subsequently was found guilty by court-martial of dereliction of duty.

To add to the desolation and discomfort of my position, the road was straight as an arrow, and could be traced, both in front and rear, as far as the eye could reach; while a rank dense vegetation crept along the foot of the swampy and monotonous line of wood closely skirting what had been a highway, and forcibly impressing me with the belief that its only tenants could be the most slimy of the creeping tribe.

I was now, I knew, not far from a scene which had been endeared to my young recollection, yet which since my boyhood I have never had an opportunity of approaching:—this was the spot on which the great Indian chief, Tecumseh, had fallen; and where I, with the greatest part of my regiment had, as I have before remarked, been captured by the Americans. The "forty mile woods," through which I had just passed, had been celebrated, at that period, for the pursuit through it, by a party of mounted Kentuckians, of the General who commanded us, [General Procter] and who had basely deserted his men at the very commencement of the action. On emerging from this, I, for the first time, beheld the Indian village, situated in a small plain, whither it had been the original intention to move the army and our Indian allies—some three thousand warriors—in order that we might take up a position from which the enemy could not easily have dislodged us, protected as we should have been by the river (Thames) on the left flank, by a morass on the right, and by a ravine in front. But weightier considerations had prevented the carrying into effect of this excellent plan of arrangement, by which an entire division of the army might have been saved, and much injury and annoyance spared to the subjugated country. It had, unfortunately, happened that the waggons containing the General's kitchen utensils, and other "plunder," as a genuine Yankee would have termed it, had not been able to get beyond this point in the line of retreat, when the enemy were announced as coming rapidly up to us. Here was a perplexity, and what was to be done to extricate the endangered culinary and other domestic household goods? Pots and kettles and frying-pans were not to be found everywhere in those times of scarcity, and it was deemed advisable to cover their retreat at all hazards. The plan of defence was therefore changed. The *batterie de cuisine* was forthwith put in motion, while the troops received the order to halt where they were, and form two extended lines in a forest which rendered them a most easy prey to the enemy, while the latter moved among the trees and foliage almost unseen by their less practised adversaries. But although what men were not knocked on the head were made prisoners in defending the approach to the General's main battery—the aforesaid *batterie de cuisine*—this latter did not the less fall into the hands of the triumphant enemy who, had the party pursuing succeeded in capturing their gallant proprietor, would, without a doubt, have cut him to pieces and boiled him in one of his largest saucepans.

As I passed from the plain into the wood where we had been attacked, I anxiously sought to discover any traces of the particular ground on which we had rested. For this purpose I alighted from my waggon, leaving the reins in the hands of my tiger; but in vain did I seek any indication of the precise spot. The general features of the wood bore so monotonous a resemblance that I was completely at fault, and after a fruitless attempt to discover the grave which was said to contain the bones of the well-known but unfortunate Tecumseh, I moved along the road which I had last traversed as a prisoner of war, in the hands of an exasperated and insulting enemy with feelings deeply imbued with painful recollections of the occurrences of that eventful day. There was no one who could point out to me the grave of the indomitable warrior who had sealed his faith to England, and his unbending determination to avenge the great and manifold wrongs of his oppressed race, with his heart's blood, and I felt deeply disappointed. I had known Tecumseh well. During my boyhood he had ever treated me as a young favorite, and I had experienced a good deal of pride in what I considered a very great condescension, for I had always entertained a deep and enthusiastic admiration of his generous, fearless, independent and warlike character. Not an hour before he fell, he had passed along our line in the elegant deer-skin frock, fringed, and ornamented with the stained quills of the porcupine, which he usually wore, and which, on this occasion, surmounted a shirt of snowy whiteness. In addition to this, he wore a plume of white ostrich feathers, and the whole style of his costume was such as to impart to his dark features an expression, and to his eagle eye a brilliancy, which the excitement of the occasion rendered even more remarkable, and which had been so forcibly impressed upon my memory, that whenever the image of the noble Indian has appeared to me, it has been as he then looked, when, for the last time, he cordially shook me by the hand.

[Here Richardson again takes up the subject of R. M. Johnson's killing of Tecumseh and his correspondence with Johnson to elicit a confirmation. In his reply Johnson refrains from "all illusion to the matter" which Richardson regards as "the modesty of truth."]

About a mile beyond the scene of action, I came to a house which had ever been vividly impressed on my memory, by reason of a ludicrous circumstance which had occurred in it the day after our defeat and capture. When our baggage was overtaken and stopped by the enemy, our own women were the first to plunder it, so that the linen of the officers adorned some of these Amazons in much greater profusion than it did those of our tall Kentuckian captors. On the morning following the action, we were marched back to the house to which I have alluded—a sort of inn, which was kept by one Sherman—and were warming ourselves by a stove in the apartment into which we had been ushered, when some eight or ten of our soldiers' wives unceremoniously entered and threw themselves into chairs, while they unblushingly displayed some of the trophies they had obtained, coolly asking us at the same time if we would purchase them. Now, under ordinary circumstances, the appearance of these women among us would scarcely have been regarded as an intrusion; but as we were fully sensible, from their manner, that they were desirous of insulting us in our altered position as prisoners, the impertinence was not to be tolerated. One officer in particular remonstrated with them, and commanded that they should leave the room instantly, but this order, so far from being obeyed, called forth all the billingsgate powers of the ladies. They jumped up, snapped their fingers, put their hands on their hips, and favored the offender with such a volley of "slang" as had never before greeted his ears, politely intimating that they would be d—d if they left the room for "such as we were," who stood in the same position with themselves, being only prisoners and without any power to compel them. And thus they went on, until the uproar terminated, not in their expulsion, but in our withdrawal from the reach of the venom of their tongues. Often and often since had that scene occurred to me, and the very position of the house in which it had taken place was so forcibly impressed upon my recollection that I recognised it at a glance. As I looked up at the sign—which doubtless had continued to hang there since I last passed the spot—I beheld the same name—Sherman—half visible in the dimness of a paint that had perhaps been washed by a thousand rains, and every feature of the dwelling was precisely what my memory had retained.

By inserting documentation and omitting the story of his imprisonment in Kentucky in his *War of 1812*, Richardson gave his book the look of an official history but weakened it of the interest of a continuous narrative and the personality of the narrator. The parliament of the newly united Canada West and East voted to grant him the money to write the war experiences of the Centre and Left Divisions to add to this account of the Right Division, but public interest was negligible and the Education Department under pressure from the Reform Party, concerned about upsetting the Americans, withdrew its offer to select the volumes for its schools. Richardson invested the money in a newspaper which he published in Kingston to revive conservative political interests: *The Canadian Loyalist and Spirit of 1812*.

Richardson's imprisonment served as a source of inspiration for his novel *The Canadian Brothers* and, also, as a starting point for his first novel, *Ecarté; or, The Salons of Paris*. In *The Canadian Don Quixote; the Life and Works of Major John Richardson,* I have described in more detail some of the persons he met in Kentucky, to which I refer you.

The writing of a memoir was becoming increasingly popular as a literary form following Jean-Jacques Rousseau's *Confessions* which appeared about twenty-five years earlier. Richardson's graphic description of fighting and dying in war, its wantonness of destruction, its savagery as witnessed through the actions of the American Indian, and the lack of concern of the generals for the welfare of their troops and their poor decisions must have riveted the attention of the English reader, whose newspapers had made him aware of certain massacres during the American Revolution. Moreover, there was a curiosity in England about the American Indian that would make such a piece popular with many readers. The editor of the *New Monthly Magazine*, Thomas Campbell wrote the poem "Gertrude of Wyoming" describing the massacre of settlers in the Wyoming Valley during the Revolutionary War and therefore was predisposed to publishing Richardson's essay. Campbell did little of the editing work, however, and left the running of the magazine in the capable hands of Cyrus Redding.

Little comment need be made on the essay, for it speaks for itself. Richardson's comment as the prisoners were moved out of Chillicothe after being accused of planning to burn the town requires a correction. Richardson wrote, "From more than one of these [young ladies at the windows] the occasional and partial movement of a handkerchief or hand waved an adieu, which seemed apprehensive of detection; but manacled as we were, the eye alone could reply to the salutation." He took the gesture as one of discreet sympathy; what he did not know was that the waving of a handkerchief in the Ohio of that day was an expression of derision. However, the waving of hands in some instances may have indicated a woman's sympathy and shown that not all were fooled by the propaganda of the authorities.

The young Richardson's experiences as a boy soldier [he was 15 when he became a Gentleman Volunteer, 17 when a prisoner] gave him insight into the motives of people, made him ready to defend his honor, as an officer must always do, and gave him material for the sudden, violent and duplicitous actions in his novels. He made close friends in the military—some of whom he depicted in his novel set at the time of the War, *The Canadian Brothers*—with whom he stayed in contact throughout his life. In 1846 at a low moment and beset by creditors, Richardson defended the 41st Regiment from recent criticism and wrote of the "splendid grenadier or light company." "The battalion men were fine fellows also, but the flank companies were really superb. Tall, well-built, fearless, careless, full of life, and activity, and union—eager ever to come in contact with the enemy—they were the impersonations of the excellence of the British soldier; and many a handsome cheek and manly form meets my eye in imagination, and with startling fidelity, at this remote period of time, and many a joyous laugh rings in recollection upon my ear, as I pass in mental review those gallant fellows, most of whose bones lie rotting, not in Canada, but on the American soil. Peace be to the ashes of the noble fellows, to whose memory I am not ashamed to confess I even now, while penning this paragraph, drop an involuntary tear."[2] The officers were "remarkable, for the manliness and elegance of their appearance;" he named sixteen of them with great fondness. He wrote in his *War of 1812*: "The Right Division were not long suffered to remain inactive—Like Sir Thomas Picton's famous division in Spain, they might, on a much more modest and limited scale, have been termed the fighting division of Canada. No other corps was so incessantly in the field—no other corps achieved such important and beneficial results to the country, and when it is considered that this force comprised scarcely more than a single regiment of the line, the repeated

---

[2] *Major Richardson's Major-General Sir Isaac Brock and the 41st Regiment*, ed T.B. Higginson (Burks Falls, Old Rectory, 1976).

claims made upon its energies and exertions, becomes even more remarkable."

Richardson gave a list of the officers imprisoned with him in Frankfort in his *War of 1812*:

"Lieut.-Col. Warburton—Major Chambers, D.A.Q.M.G.—Major Muir, 41st—Captain Derenzy, do—Capt. McCoy, do—Capt. Hill, do—Capt. Tallon, do—Capt. Dixon, Royal Engineers—Lieut. Hailes, 4lst—Lieut. Watson, do—Lieut. Linn, do—Lieut. Jeboult, do—Lieut. O'Keefe, do—Lieut. Gale, do—Lieut. Purvis, Royal Navy—Lieut. Stokoe, do—Lieut. Bremner, Provincial do—Lieut, Rolette, do—Lieut. Irvine, do—Lieut. Holmes, Light Dragoons—Ensign Mompesson, 41st—Ensign Cochran, do—Ensign Jones, do—A. B. Garden, Gent. Volunteer, Royal Newfoundland Regt.—J. Richardson, do. 4lst—James Laing, do—J. Campbell, Master's Mate, R.P.N.—G. Collins, do—J. Fortier, do—R, Nelson, Midshipman.
The whole number of prisoners were about 900, including those taken on the lake."

Richardson's enthusiasm for the military led him to remain on active service in the United Kingdom when many regiments were demobilized after Napoleon was defeated. He served in the West Indies from 1816 to late 1818 when he went to half-pay and returned to London. It was the beginning of his disillusionment with the army as his "Recollections of the West Indies" reveals. My comments on it follow the piece. By the time he served the British Auxiliary Legion in Spain, he became disgusted with the new kind of officer whose goals were promotion for social standing and some adventure which was not too dangerous. I add my essay "In Search of Richardson's Spain" as a digression on that period of his life, though for a full description of his tumultuous time in the Legion and its aftermath, one should read the appropriate chapters in *The Canadian Don Quixote*.

The Canadian historian Ernest Cruikshank identified the anonymous "A Canadian Campaign" as Richardson's in an article on Richardson's *War of 1812* in volume 7 [1902/03] of the *Review of Historical Publications Relating to Canada*, edited by G. M. Wrong. Richardson acknowledged it in his poem *Tecumseh* issued in 1828.

A CANADIAN CAMPAIGN,
BY A BRITISH OFFICER

No. 1

THIS narrative is intended rather as a private memoir than a relation of the incidents of the war, and professes simply to detail the operations of the right division of the British army in Upper Canada, to which I was myself attached, together with its capture and imprisonment (in October 1813) without following in progression the movements of the various other corps. I have not gone, therefore, into a diffuse statement of every date and circumstance, which would necessarily encroach too much on the plan I have laid down, as calculated to afford a source of interest to the general reader, rather than a fund from whence minute information for a diffusive work may be obtained.

Much has been said and written in respect to the American Indians; but I do not recollect having ever met with a detail sufficiently accurate to convey a just idea of the character of these people. As they will occupy a tolerable portion of my attention, and frequently appear under circumstances which might incline the reader to incredulity, I will merely observe, that no one incident will be found committed to these pages, which may not be attested by every officer who served with the right division of the Canadian army. In fact, to that division alone were the more savage of the Indian race attached; and when it is considered, that among the warriors of at least twenty different tribes, there were those who had scarcely ever any previous intercourse with whites, and had seldom approached a fortified place but in open hostility, the savageness of their natures will cease to excite surprise. As it is my intention to give a faithful account of the various cruelties committed during our struggle in Canada—cruelties we had not power to prevent, since perpetrated by an ally over whom we had no control—it may not be improper to advert to the motives for their employment. The

Americans have invariably been loud in their condemnation of a measure which alone secured to us the possession of Upper Canada: with how little reason, however, will appear from the well-known fact, that every possible exertion was used, by the agents of their Government, to detach the Indians from our cause. Embracing the system adopted and followed by England for years, presents of all descriptions were issued to the warriors; while, in the council, the most flattering promises were made, the most seducing offers held forth, to induce them to make common cause with the invader. The wary chieftains, however, were not to be tempted by professions of friendship from those whose perfidy had long been proverbial with the Indian race. The bounties of England had been heaped on them with no sparing hand—the faith of the Government had never been violated—no spirit of interest or dominion had chased them from the homes of their forefathers—the calumet of peace had never once been dashed from the lips of those they were called on to abandon; and they remained true to the faith they had pledged, staunch to the cause in which they had embarked. The natives must have been our friends or our foes: had we not employed them the Americans would; and although humanity may deplore the necessity imposed by the very invader himself, of counting them among our allies, and combatting at their side,—the law of self-preservation was our guide, and scrupulous indeed must be the power that would have hesitated at such a moment in its choice. The act of aggression was not ours—we declared no war against America—we levied no armies to invade her soil, and carry desolation wherever they came:—but we availed ourselves of that right, common to every weak power—the right of repelling acts of aggression by every means within our reach. Yet though it is admitted that the Indians, while our allies, were in some instances guilty of those atrocities peculiar to every savage people; let it not be supposed, as has been falsely and maliciously stated in a work from the pen of an "Englishwoman," that these atrocities were sanctioned either by the Government or by individuals. On the contrary, every possible mean was tried by the officer commanding at Amherstburg, and Colonel Elliott, superintendent of Indian affairs for that post, to soften down the warlike habits of the natives. The most likely method of preventing the unnecessary effusion of blood was that of offering rewards for prisoners. This, however, except in a very few instances, was found to be ineffectual; for the character and disposition of the savage were not to be tamed by rewards, nor the impression of ages to be removed by such temptations. To have employed force, would have been to have turned their weapons against ourselves; and a body or eight hundred troops, composing the utmost strength of the garrison, could have effected little against three thousand fiery warriors, unused to restraint, and acknowledging no power but their own lawless and unbridled will. The Americans themselves had Indians employed in their service—a few only it is true —but if they had not more, it was not owing to any want of exertion on their parts; and if it is admitted on one hand, that they conducted themselves with more humanity, it cannot at the same time be denied on the other, that the feebleness of their numbers rendered them more immediately subject to the authority of the American commanders, neither, can it, be disputed, that compulsion alone bound them to the adverse cause, their families having been often detained as hostages to answer for their fidelity.

The garrison of Amherstburg, at the commencement of the war, consisted merely of a part of the first battalion of the 41st regiment, and a single company of artillery. Situated at the head of Lake Erie, and forming the key to our relations with the Western Indians, with whom an extensive and lucrative trade in furs had long been established by the North-West Company, this post became an object of additional interest to the enemy. With every opportunity of ascertaining the weakness of its defences, and the almost utter impossibility of its obtaining supplies, the fall of Amherstburg was looked forward to by the Americans, as an event which admitted not of doubt. With this view, the division under General Hull, consisting of three thousand men, had been urged forward with all possible despatch to Detroit, a fort established on the river of the same name, and at a distance of eighteen miles beyond Amherstburg, an attack on which latter place was immediately contemplated. Having collected his boats, and made every other necessary preparation, the American general effected his landing three miles above Sandwich, a small town nearly opposite to Detroit, and within view of a corps of observation, which, in conformity with its instructions, retired on his approach. Colonel (now Major-General) St. George, Inspecting Field-officer, and then commanding at Amherslburg, with that spirit and activity by which he was distinguished throughout the war, made every judicious disposition for his reception. The militia were called out, and, through the exertions of the various agents of their department, a body of one thousand Indians were soon collected. At a distance of eight miles from Amherstburg, and traversing the high road, is the Duck River, which empties itself into that of the Detroit, and is impassable even by cavalry. Over this, and near its mouth, a bridge composed entirely of timber, had been constructed. Seizing at once the advantage of this position, and determined to profit by the delay the enemy must consequently experience, Colonel St. George instantly caused the bridge to be destroyed, and a body of marksmen to be posted among the long grass and weeds with which the banks of the river are covered, for the purpose of annoying such of the enemy as appeared for its reconstruction. The Queen Charlotte, a vessel of twenty guns, was at the same times anchored at the mouth of the river, for the purpose of keeping them more effectually in check.

The activity with which General Hull commenced his offensive operations gave every possible indication that they would be followed with vigour, and that, having once effected his landing, he would afford no time for his enemies to collect the few resources they could command, or place themselves in a posture of defence. The fort of Amherstburg could not have sustained a siege of any consequence. Quadrangular in its form, four bastions alone flanked by a dry ditch, offering little obstacle to a determined enemy. This passed, a single file of picketing, perforated with loopholes for musketry, and supported by a slight breast-work, remained to be carried. A prudent commander would, however, have chosen a less uncertain mode of dislodging the garrison. A few shells properly directed would have answered the purpose, since, with the exception of the magazine, all the buildings within were of wood, and covered with pine shingles of such extreme thinness, as would have been found incapable of resisting missiles of far less weight.

The disadvantage of awaiting the enemy in this position, Colonel St. George well knew; and consequently preferred giving him battle with the trifling force he had at his disposition. With this view, the garrison received orders to be under arms at a moment's warning, and the approach of the invader was anxiously awaited. Satisfied, however, with having effected his landing, and deriving no other advantage than that of having his troops quartered on his enemy, the American general appeared to have forgotten altogether the object of his mission. Instead of descending the River Detroit in boats, or attempting to throw a bridge across the other river at a point where we had no outpost, he contented himself with despatching workmen, supported by bodies of cavalry and infantry, to repair that already partially destroyed. Repulsed in every attempt, the daily skirmishes which ensued led to no action of a decisive nature. Each party sustained a trifling loss; the enemy invariably retiring at the approach of evening. In this manner passed the whole of the latter end of July, when suddenly, and to the utter astonishment of the garrison, intelligence was received that the enemy had recrossed the River Detroit, with the whole of his force.

On the 6th of August, information haying been conveyed to Colonel St. George, that a body of the enemy was on its march to convoy a quantity of provisions for the use of the garrison of Detroit, Brevet-Major Muir, with a detachment of a hundred and fifty men of the forty-first regiment, and a few companies of militia, received orders to cross the river and occupy Brownstown, a small village on the American shore through which they were expected to pass. On our arrival at this post, we found that their advanced guard had fallen in with, and been defeated by a party of Indians a few hours before, and that the main body had in consequence retired with much precipitation on Detroit.

It was on this occasion that one of those cruel practices, common to the Indian race, fell for the first time beneath the observation of the indignant soldiery. Their horror at the atrocious act was such as might naturally be expected from men, to whose humanity the voice of a suppliant foe had never been used to tender an ineffectual appeal. Among the number of those who had fallen in the morning, was a young Shawanee chief named Logan, killed by almost the last shot fired from the enemy. Speaking the English language with facility, he was known to many of the officers, with whom his mild and unassuming nature had rendered him a great favourite, and he was sincerely regretted by all. Shortly after our arrival, the body of the warrior was brought in, and placed in a large tent, where it was immediately surrounded by the female relatives. It is customary with the Indians when a man falls in battle, either to fill up the void his decease occasions in the family by the adoption of a prisoner, or to sacrifice one to his shade. While the howling and lamentation of the women were at their height, two Indians suddenly appeared with a captive, who, in his attempt to extricate himself from the woods in which he had lost during the affair of the morning, had fallen into their hands. He was a finely proportioned young man, and the air of dejection which clouded his brow, gradually gave way to a more cheerful expression, when, on approaching the encampment, he perceived those from whom he expected protection. Several of the men advanced to meet and converse with him, and the poor fellow had apparently banished all feeling of apprehension for his future fate, when an aunt of the deceased issued from the tent and stole cautiously behind him. She was a tall, thin woman, with a fiend-like expression of countenance, and the fires which extreme age had taken from her eye, were for a moment rekindled by the spirit of demonic vengeance that trembled throughout her frame. Even at the moment when the mind of the prisoner was most lulled into confidence, and without any previous admonition, the heartless woman drew a tomahawk from beneath her mantle, and buried its point in the skull of her victim. Stunned but not felled by the wound, the unhappy man—his whole countenance expressing horror and despair—grasped at the first soldier near him for support; but the blows were repeated so suddenly, and with such violence, that he soon fell panting and convulsive to the earth. Fortunately he was not suffered to linger in his agony. The Indians around instantly despatched and scalped him, stripping the body of its clothes, and committing violations on his person which it would be indecent to detail, and in which the cruel aunt of Logan bore a principal share, The indignation of the men was excessive; but any attempt to interfere, could they even have foreseen the occurrence in time to render interference effectual, would not only have cost them several lives, but produced the most alarming consequences to our cause. Their displeasure was, however, expressed by their murmurs, and the atrocity of the act became the theme of conversation throughout the camp. At the moment of its perpetration, I had myself approached within a few paces of the group, and became an unwilling spectator of the whole transaction. The wild expression of the sufferer's eye; the supplicating look which spoke through the very distortion of his features; and the agony which seemed to creep throughout his every limb, were such as no time can ever efface from my recollection. It was but the work of a moment, yet, although it has been my melancholy fortune to witness many other scenes of an equally cruel character, I can recall none that affected me in the same degree. Human nature is, perhaps, in some measure to be taxed for this apparent inconsistency, since sad experience has too long taught us, that the horror with which we are inspired at the sight of crime or cruelty will yield to the influence of habit, and that the eye which, in the infancy of its communion with blood, shrank back from the contemplation of atrocity, will eventually dwell with comparative calm on all that is outrageous and disgusting to humanity. Each particular circumstance is present to my mind as though it had been an occurrence of yesterday, and I will venture to believe, that there are few of those who were also involuntary eye-witnesses of a deed they had not the power to prevent, who have not retained an equally melancholy impression of a crime in the perpetration of which the principal agent and Instrument was a woman!

On the morning of the 9th the wild and distant cry or our Indian scouts gave us to understand that the enemy were advancing. In the course of ten minutes afterwards they appeared issuing from the wood, bounding like wild deer chased by the huntsman, and uttering that peculiar shout which is known among themselves as the news-cry. From them we ascertained that a column of the enemy, consisting of eight hundred men, cavalry and infantry, were on their march to attack us, but that the difficulty of transporting their guns rendered it improbable they could reach our position before night, although then only at a distance or eight miles. It being instantly decided on to meet them, the detachment was speedily under arms, and on its march for Miguaga, a small village distant about a league. The road along which we advanced was ankle-deep with mud, and the dark forest waving its close branches over our heads, left no egress to the pestilential exhalations arising from the naked and putrid bodies of horses and men, which had been suffered to lie unburied beneath our feet. No other sound than the measured step of the troops interrupted the solitude of the scene, rendered more imposing by the wild appearance of the warriors, whose bodies, stained and painted in the most frightful manner for the occasion, glided by us with almost noiseless velocity, without order, and without a chief: some painted white, some black, others half black half red, half black, half white, all with their hair plastered in such a way as to resemble the bristling quills of the porcupine, with no other covering than a cloth around their loins, yet armed to the teeth with rifles, tomahawks, war-clubs, spears, bows. arrows and scalping-knives. Uttering no sound, and intent only on reaching the enemy unperceived, they might have passed for the spectres of those wilds the ruthless demons which War had unchained for the punishment and oppression of man.

Having taken up a position at about a quarter of a mile beyond Miguaga, our dispositions of defence were speedily made, the rustling of the leaves alone breaking on the silence which reigned throughout our line. Following the example of the Indians, we lay reclined on the ground, in order to avoid being perceived until within a few yards of the enemy. At the expiration of an hour the report of a single shot echoed throughout the wood; and the instant afterwards the loud and terrific yells of the Indians, followed by a heavy and desultory fire, apprised us that they were engaged. The action then became general along our line, and continued for half an hour, without producing any material advantage; when, unluckily, a body of Indians that had been detached to a small wood about five hundred yards distant from our right, were taken by the troops for a corps of the enemy endeavouring to turn their flank. In vain we called out to them that they were our Indians. That fire which should have been reserved for their foes, was turned upon their friends, who, falling into the same error, returned it with equal spirit. The fact was, they had been compelled to retire before a superior force, and the movement made by them had given rise to the error of the troops. That order and discipline which would have marked their conduct as a body in a plain, was lost sight of, in a great measure, while fighting independently and singly in a wood, where every man, following the example of the enemy, was compelled to shelter his person behind the trees as he could. Closely pressed in front by an almost invisible foe, and on the point of being taken in the rear, as was falsely imagined, the troops were at length compelled to yield to circumstance and numbers; the Americans suffering us to retire without molestation to our boats, in which we the same evening regained the Fort of Amherstburg.

This affair, the first that took place since our rupture with America cost us Lieutenant Sutherland of the 41st regiment, and about twenty men. The loss of the enemy we subsequently found to have been nearly the same, and principally sustained from the fire of the Indians. Here it was that we had first an opportunity of perceiving the extreme disadvantage of opposing regular troops to the enemy in the woods. Accustomed to the use of the rifle from his infancy—dwelling in a measure amid forests with the intricacies of which he is perfectly acquainted, and possessing the advantage of a dress which renders him almost undistinguishable to the eye of an European, the American marksman enters with comparative security into a contest with the English soldier, whose glaring habiliment and accoutrement are objects too conspicuous to be missed, while his utter ignorance of a mode of warfare, in which courage and discipline are of no avail, renders the struggle for mastery even more unequal. The different armies to which the right division was opposed during the war, consisted not of regular and well-disciplined troops, but levies of men taken from the forests of Ohio and Kentucky, scarcely inferior as riflemen to the Indians themselves. Dressed in woolen frocks of a gray colour, and trained to cover their bodies behind the trees from which they fired, without exposing more of their persons than was absolutely necessary for their aim, they afforded us, on more than one occasion, the most convincing proofs that without the assistance of the Indian warriors, the defence of that part of Upper Canada entrusted to our care would have been a task of the utmost difficulty and doubt.

Major-General Brock having reinforced the garrison of Amherstburg early in the following week, with the remainder of the 41st regiment, and a few companies of the York militia, resolved at one bold and desperate stroke to attempt the annihilation of the enemy's power in the Western District. With this view batteries were instantly erected opposite to the fort of Detroit, and the whole of his disposable force marched with the utmost expedition to Sandwich. At day-break on the morning of the 16th, the troops were embarked in boats and canoes of every description, covered by the flotilla under the command of Captain Hall. Meeting with no opposition, and forming on the beach as they landed, the columns were soon within view of the enemy's works, then occupied in returning the heavy and well-directed fire from our batteries. Arrived within a few hundred paces, a position was taken up on an eminence, and the various columns disposed for a general assault. Our whole force consisted of about 1200 men, exclusive of the Indians, and a few pieces of light artillery. While awaiting the order to advance, a white flag was suddenly seen waving on the ramparts of the citadel, and in less than two hours the divisions moved forward to take possession of the garrison which had surrendered. Every mind was filled with astonishment at the event:—a place strongly fortified, defended by five and thirty pieces of cannon, and garrisoned by 3500 men, thus falling into our possession, without a single shot being fired—without the slightest effort being made for its defence, was certainly a circumstance to excite surprise; nor was the general satisfaction less, since with its capture not only vanished all immediate apprehension for the safety of Amhersthurg, but an important object had been obtained in the possession of a fortress, from whence every possible obstacle might be thrown to impede the march of a future invading army.

The articles of capitulation having stipulated that the troops composing the garrison of Detroit should be suffered to return to their respective homes on parole, they were immediately embarked, and sent down the lake to Buffalo, the nearest American post, and opposite to our small fortress of Erie. Leaving a garrison sufficiently strong to keep the inhabitants in awe, General Brock lost no time in leaving the conquered post, and hastening to Niagara—a command he had only relinquished for the purpose of undertaking an achievement which the gallantry and determination of his character could alone have crowned with such unqualified success.

The prisoners having been landed at Buffalo, the flotilla returned to Amherstburg, leaving in the harbour of Erie the brig Adams, captured at Detroit, pierced for eighteen guns, but mounting merely a few swivels at the moment, ad manned by a handful of men, together with the merchant brig Caledonia, the property of Mr. Angus Mackintosh, and commanded by Mr. Irvine, a young gentleman about two-and-twenty, but possessed of a coolness of character far beyond his years. The Americans having collected a number of seamen at Buffalo, and ascertaining from the prisoners just landed the inefficient state of those vessels, formed the design of cutting them out under cover of the night. Having accordingly chosen a favourable moment, and assailed by the extreme darkness, several boats with muffled oars approached within pistol-shot before they were discovered. The negligent sentinels, having at length given the alarm, the crews flew to their arms, but not in time to reach them before the enemy had leaped on the deck of the Adams, which thus became an easy conquest. The only resistance offered was on the part of Mr. Irvine, who, having his vessel anchored at some distance beyond, was thus enabled on the first alarm to return to his cabin for arms. Upon reappearing on deck, a boat was discovered within a few yards of the Caledonia, and, receiving no reply to his hail, Mr. Irvine discharged a blunderbuss with murderous effect amid the crew. To the summons to surrender which ensued, he only replied by a second and equally effectual discharge, succeeded by that of his pistols; nor did he cease to defend himself until the enemy had actually gained the deck, when a severe wound from a cutlass in the head, in depriving him of sensation, left no farther opposition to the assailants, who carried their prizes triumphantly into Buffalo.

The gallantry and self-devotion of Mr. Irvine, whose single arm had destroyed seven of the enemy, met with those encomiums to which they were so justly entitled. The heads of the naval department, anxious to secure so promising an officer to the service, tendered him on his exchange, which took place shortly after, the commission of a lieutenant, in which capacity he continued to serve until the conclusion of the war.

The fall of Detroit having secured the tranquillity of Amherstburg and its contiguous districts, an expedition was projected to the interior of the enemy's country, the object of which was the destruction of Fort Wayne, a post distant several hundred miles, and serving as a depot for stores, from which the various troops of the enemy pushed forward to the frontier were supplied. The garrison, according to the intelligence received, consisted merely of a few hundred men, and several pieces of cannon indifferently mounted. Towards the close of September a detachment of troops, a howitzer, and two field pieces, under the command of Brevet Major Muir, were embarked in boats, and proceeded across the lake to the Miami village, situated about fifteen miles beyond the entrance of the river of the same name. Being there joined by the body of Indians destined to form a part of the expedition, the detachment continued its route by land, and along a tract of country bearing no mark of civilization whatever. The only covering at night was the canopy of Heaven, or rather the arches formed by the intermingling boughs of the forest through which we moved, and not even the hut of tbe savage arose to diversify the monotony of the scene. The difficulty of conveying the guns by land caused their transportation to be a work of much time; and the river from the point where we had disembarked was so extremely low, as to render the progress of the boats following the sinuosities of its course tedious to the last degree. Having at length, after much toil, gained that part of the Miami, where it was intended to disembark the stores, every obstacle appeared to be removed, and the capture of Fort Wayne, then at no great distance, an event looked forward to with confidence. Fate, however, had ordained otherwise. About nine o'clock on the evening of our arrival, the piercing cry of our scouts was heard echoing throughout the forest, and soon afterwards seven Indians issued from the wood on the opposite shore, and, leaping through the river, reached our encampment with the scalps of several Americans. The account they gave of their adventure was to the following effect. At a distance of a few leagues, while advancing cautiously along the road, they observed a party, five in number, in a glen, and seated round a large fire, where they were busily occupied in preparing their food. After a slight consultation they proceeded towards the group, and had approached within a few paces before they were perceived by the Americans, who instantly flew to their arms, and assumed a posture of defence. The artful natives, however, held out their hands in token of amity, and were suffered to enter the circle. Here, pretending to be in the American interest, and describing themselves as hunters on their way to one of their villages, they succeeded in lulling the suspicions of the officer, who in return communicated to them that the party he commanded were scouts preceding the advanced guard of an army of two thousand five hundred men, then on its march for the Miami village, and only distant a few miles. This disclosure obtained, the Indians, satisfied that they had no time to lose, and throwing of the mask, desired them to deliver up their arms. The astonished party thus entrapped, and unwilling to risk a contest with a superior force, consented to accompany them as their prisoners, but positively refused to relinquish their rifles, They all therefore proceeded in silence towards our encampment, three Indians on each flank of their prisoners, and one in the rear. On the approach of evening the Americans were again desired to deliver up their rifles, and on refusing to do so, at a signal given by one of the Indians, the whole of his party dropped, one by one, and apparently without premeditation, behind. Each then selected his victim, and four of those unhappy men fell to rise no more. The officer alone, slightly wounded, made an ineffectual attempt to escape, but, closely pursued through the intricacies of the forest by two of his merciless foes. He was at length overtaken, and felled to the earth by a blow from a tomahawk. This cruel scene must have taken place at no great distance from our encampment, the shots having been distinctly heard about half an hour before the appearance of the Indians, who, on being questioned, excused the treachery of their conduct, under the plea of the Americans being nearly equal in numbers to themselves, and obstinately refusing to deliver up their arms, circumstances which rendered their destruction at the approach of evening a measure of self-security—especially so, as having been sent in advance four of five days before, they were not aware of our being encamped at so short a distance.

No. II

In consequence of the foregoing intelligence, all idea of continuing the expedition against Fort Wayne was abandoned, and the boats were ordered the same evening to descend the river. Major Muir having, however, resolved to await the approach of the enemy, a position was taken up early on the following morning on the heights overlooking the ford at which the Americans were expected to cross. Having passed the whole of the day in the vain expectation of his appearance, it was at length decided on, that the enemy apprised of our vicinity by the view of the bodies of their scouts slain the evening before, had taken a different direction, and instead of traversing the river at the usual ford, had forced their march by a less frequented route on the opposite shore. Such a manoeuvre on the part of the American general would necessarily have cut off our retreat, and we must have combated an enemy infinitely superior in numbers, under every disadvantage, in the heart of his own country and, in the event of our boats falling into his hands, destitute of every resource. The detachment was consequently ordered to retire on the old fort of Defiance, situated about half way between the Miami village and the point from whence we commenced our retreat, formerly garrisoned by the British troops, during the celebrated Pontiac war, so fatally waged against us by the confederated tribes of Indians, but then in a state of utter ruin and dilapidation. Having crossed the river at this place, a position was again taken up at a point beyond which the enemy could not effect his passage unperceived. Here, however, we did not long remain. Early on the morning after our arrival, a party of Indians appeared along our line, conducting a prisoner they had found straying in the woods, at a short distance from the enemy's camp. From his account it appeared that the information given by the American officer was perfectly correct. The force of the enemy consisted of 2,500 men, under the command of General Winchester; and were destined for the

Miami, where it was intended to construct a fortification. On arriving at the spot where their slaughtered scouts lay unburied along the road, an alarm was spread throughout their columns, and deeming a numerous enemy to be in their front, it was thought prudent to entrench themselves where they were. For this purpose trees were immediately felled, and in the course of a few hours, with that expedition for which the Western Americans, with whom the axe is almost as indispensable a weapon as the rifle, are remarkable, an enclosure with interstices for musquetry, and sufficiently large to contain their whole force, together with their baggage and waggons, was completed. It being evident from this intelligence, that the object of our enterprise was entirely frustrated, and that an attack on the enemy's entrenchment with our feeble force, if unsuccessful, must necessarily compromise the safety of our own posts. Major Muir decided on returning to Amherstburg, which fortress the detachment at length reached after a fruitless absence of three weeks.

In the course of our return, and shortly subsequent to his capture, we fell in with the prisoner from whom the above report had been obtained. He was already adopted in that tribe of Indians, to which his captors belonged, and was habited after their manner. His head was partly shaved, and covered with a handerkerchief, rolled in the form of a turban, after the manner of the natives. His face was painted several colors, and so complete was the metamorphosis, that but for the whiteness of skin visible through several parts of his dress, it would have been difficult to distinguish him from those by whom he was surrounded. At the moment we saw him, he was seated in a tent, sharing the evening meal of his new countrymen, with much appetite and unconcern. He expressed himself as being quite reconciled to his new condition, and spoke with warmth of the kind treatment he had received; nor did he seem to attach much consequence to the assurance given him that every exertion would be made on our return to obtain his liberation. We saw him some weeks later at Amherstburg; and strange as it may appear, he assured us that he preferred the idle life he had led among the Indians, to a repetition of active service in the American army.

About this period Mr. Robert Dickson, a gentleman to whom a long intercourse with the more remote savages of the West had rendered their language and customs as familiar as his influence among them was unbounded, arrived at Amherstburg with a number of canoes, filled with warriors of the fiercest character and appearance. Among the most remarkable of these tribes were the Sawkies, a race of men, whose towering height, athletic forms, and nobleness of feature, might recall the idea of the Romans in the earlier stages of their barbarity; and another tribe, whose Indian name I do not recollect, but who were known among ourselves by their assumed appellation of devoted men. The costume of the latter was a dress of white leather, extremely pliant, and curiously embroidered with the stained quills of the porcupine, in the preparation of which the natives evince much taste and ingenuity. They were few in number, and, professing to hold death in derision, were looked upon by the other warriors much in the same light that we regard our forlorn hope, the post of danger being reserved for them. One of their chiefs, having been invited to breakfast with several officers of the garrison, was at much pains, in the course of the meal, to impress upon the minds of his hosts the particular virtues of his tribe; and in order to demonstrate more fully the extent to which they carried their disregard of pain or death, drew a sharp knife from its sheath, and, having cut a piece of flesh out of one of his thighs, threw it contemptuously away, exclaiming that "he gave it to the dogs." A tribe even fiercer than these, although evincing no disposition to prove their hardihood and courage by the self-infliction of pain, were the Minouminies, a race of men whose limbs formed in the finest mould of symmetry, and full expansive chests, sufficiently attested to their vigour and activity. Of these, however, I shall have occasion to speak hereafter. It was a picturesque sight to behold the light bark canoes of the different warriors skimming along the surface of the broad and tranquil river of Detroit, their streamers floating in air, and the paddlers keeping time with their oars, while the salute fired from the fort, and answered from the little fleet by discharges of firearms, mingled with the shrill war-cry echoing over the bosom of the deep and dying away in the adjacent forests. The arrival of this reinforcement increased out Indian strength to three thousand warriors.

The 41st regiment, about six hundred strong, and two companies of Newfoundland Fencibles, composed the whole of our regular force. The latter were, however, employed as marines on board the different vessels of war, so that the defense of the two fortresses of Detroit and Amherstburg was entrusted to the 41st alone.

The month of October was marked by an event of the most melancholy nature—the death of General Brock, who fell a victim to the intrepidity and daring of his character. The Americans being in force along the Niagara frontier, a landing was effected early on the morning of the 13th by a considerable body under General Wadsworth, who immediately possessed himself of the heights of Queenston. The little army of General Brock consisted of the 1st battalions 8th and 49th regiments, a few companies of the Glengary Fencibles, some militia, and a small body of Indians. On the first alarm, the gallant commander, leaving General Sheaffe to bring up the main hody, dashed forward at tlle head of the flank companies of the 8th and 49th regiments, who advanced up the heights in double-quick time, and under a heavy fire from the enemy. Conspicuous from his dress, his height, and the enthusiasm with which he animated his little band, General Brock was soon recognized and singled out by their riflemen, whose celebrity for unerring aim was never more cruelly justified. Mortally wounded, he fell from his horse, and his body lay extended near that of Colonel Macdonnell, his principal aide-de-camp, a fine promising young officer, killed nearly at the same instant at his side. Filled with grief, and burning to revenge the death of their favourite commander, the men redoubled their exertions in the ascent, and the main body coming up at this moment the action became general. The enemy was soon driven from his position at the point of the bayonet. Those who attempted to escape in the woods were driven back by the Indians and militia, and falling on such of their own lines, as yet sustained the shock, threw them into confusion. Little quarter was given in the onset. Driven near the edge of the precipices, with which the Heights of Queenston abound, the enemy fought for a moment with all the obstinacy of despair, but compelled at length to yield to their exasperated foe, their remaining line was entirely broken. Many threw down their arms and implored the clemency of their victors. Others cast themselves over the precipices, and were dashed in their fall against the rocks, or hung suspended from the bushes which had caught them in their descent, and in parts where no human hand could tender them assistance. Never was victory more complete. Few of the enemy returned to tell the tale of their disaster, and the American general was among the number of captives. The loss of their leader, however, cast a gloom over the English brow, and an advantage thus purchased was deemed at too high a price. General Brock was beloved of the military, particularly the 49th, of which he had long been colonel; and the indignation of their grief for his loss cost the Americans many a life on that day, that had otherwise been spared. At Amherstburg the account of his death was received with heart-felt concern; and not a man was there of those he had led lately to victory, who failed to pay that tribute of regret to his memory, which the gallantry and magnanimity of this glorious chief was so every way calculated to awaken in the breast of the soldier.

Towards the close of autumn, General Winchester having advanced to the Miami, and thrown up a strong fortification on the right bank of that river, a detachment consisting of one hundred militia, a six-pounder, and a body of Indians, under Major Reynolds of the militia, were ordered to occupy Frenchtown, a small village on the opposite shore, situated on the river Raisin, and distant about eighteen miles from Amherstburg. Here this little corps of observation continued to remain until the 17th of January, 1813, when the advanced guard of the enemy, closely followed by their main body, suddenly appearing in sight, Major Reynolds withdrew to a small wood skirting the plain. At this point, the Americans were kept in check by an animated fire from the militia and Indians, supported by the well-directed service of Bombardier Kitson. After a spirited affair, which continued upwards of an hour, the fire from the enemy's line began to slacken, and they retired across the plain, suffering Major Reynolds to effect his retreat unmolested.

The account of this affair reaching Amherstburg on the evening of the 18th, the whole of our disposable force was ordered to be in readiness to march on the following morning. Accordingly, early on the 19th, Colonel Procter, then commanding, leaving a handful of men to garrison the posts, crossed the river Detroit with a body of one thousand troops and militia, eight hundred Indians, two howitzers, and several four and six-pounders. The different vessels, being laid up for the season, parts of their crews were ordered to serve with the artillery, and the two companies of the Newfoundland Fencibles attached to the brigade. No sight could he more beautiful than the departure of this little army from Amhersthurg. It was the depth of winter; and the river at the point we crossed being four miles in breadth, the deep rumbling noise of the guns prolonging their reverberations like the roar of distant thunder, as they moved along the ice, mingled with the wild cries of the Indians, seemed to threaten some convulsion of nature; while the appearance of the troops winding along the road, now lost behind some cliff of rugged ice, now emerging into view, their polished arms glittering in the sunbeams, gave an air of romantic grandeur to the scene, which the European unaccustomed to the sight of those stupendous seasons, can with difficulty conceive.

On the 22nd before daybreak, we came within sight of the enemy, occupying the position lately held by Major Reynolds. Such was their security and negligence, that our line was formed within musquet-shot of their defences, and yet not an individual was aware of our approach. Several shells thrown into their camp, however, soon aroused them from their slumber, and the action became general. The Americans, resting their rifles on the breastwork by which they were covered, fought under every advantage, the dark line of troops before them serving as a point of direction, which could not fail to be perceived along the tract of snow by which they were surrounded. Much execution was done among the artillery and semen. Placed in front of the lie and singled out by their marksmen, the officers and men of those departments were particularly exposed, and many of the guns were abandoned from want of hands to work them. The fire of the enemy was not less galling to the troops, yet, although falling at every step, they continued to advance with the utmost resolution and gallantry. The action had continued about an hour, when the American right being entirely broken by the militia and Indians, a movement was made to occupy the ground they had abandoned, and take the enemy in flank. This manoeuvre succeeding, a corps of

Americans, to the number of four hundred, threw themselves into the strong block-houses they had already constructed since their arrival, where they continued to make an obstinate defence. Meanwhile their right, and part of the centre, closely followed across the ice by the Indians, fell almost unresisting victims to the wrath of their pursuers: and for nearly two miles along the road by which they passed, the snow was covered with the blood and bodies of the slain. Among the fugitives was General Winchester himself, who, falling into the hands of the Wyandot Chief Roundhead, was conducted, together with his son, a handsome youth of sixteen, to our rear. Here, being informed of the state of the action, he immediately wrote an order in pencil to the officer commanding the block-houses desiring him to surrender what troops were under him as prisoners of war. This being conveyed to Colonel Procter who was then in advance with the left wing, which was fast establishing itself on the flank of the enemy's position, the fire from our line was discontinued, and an officer despatched with a flag and the document in question, the result of which was the capitulation of men, who dreading to fall into the hands of the Indians, had resolved to sell their lives at the dearest rate, and could wit difficulty have been expelled from the building into which they had thrown themselves. In this manner was the whole of the American force destroyed, one hundred and fifty men only effecting their escape into Fort Meigs, the fortification which had been erected on the banks of the Miami. So complete was the surprise of the enemy, that General Winchester, when brought in, had no other covering than the dress in which he slept, and his head was ornamented with a white cotton nightcap, which gave him a very unsoldierlike appearance indeed. It may be inquired by the military reader why, since our columns had advanced so near an enemy unconscious of their approach, they were not suffered to enter the encampment bayonet in hand, instead of being exposed unnecessarily to the destructive fire of the riflemen. That question must be resolved by those who planned the attack. Let it suffice, that the good conduct and firmness of the troops employed overcame every obstacle, and that the defeat of the enemy was of the most decisive character.

In this affair we lost twenty-five killed, and from fifty to sixty wounded of the line. The militia and Indians, having been covered by a wood and some detached fences, suffered less. Colonel St. George, particularly distinguished by his valour and exertions on this occasion, received five wounds—several of them severe, and had a horse shot under him. No officer was killed; but among the wounded were Lieutenants Carr of the Royal Newfoundland Regiment, dangerously, (since dead), Clemow, of the 41st, and Rolette and Irvine of the Navy, the latter in the heel, and immediately under the enemy's breastwork, while endeavouring singly to withdraw a four-pounder, which had been advanced and abandoned by his men. Another individual who deserves honorable mention here was a midshipman, son of Dr. Richardson of Amherstburg, one of the magistrates for that district. This youth, then only fourteen years of age, had ever been anxious to find himself engaged in an affair with the enemy, but no opportunity having presented itself on the lake, he had resolved to seize the first favorable occasion on land. Disobeying the positive order given him to remain behind, he joined the division a few hours before we reached Frenchtown, and, attaching himself to his department, was among the number of those singled out by the enemy's marksmen, and, while in the act of applying a match to one of the guns, he was struck by a ball, which shattered his right leg and felled him to the earth. Doctor Richardson had been called on in his medical capacity to attend the expedition, and was then with the staff in the rear. The first care of this gallant and excellent boy was to conceal his wound from his father; and he begged those who bore him from the field to convey him to a position remote from that occupied by the staff, and to request another surgeon to attend him, which was accordingly done. After having suffered intensely, but with manly courage, for six months, he was at length enabled to remove to Lower Canada, where, his conduct being generally known, he was taken into favour by the Commander-in-Chief, who gave him the commission of a lieutenant in one of the provincial corps. Colonel Harvey, adjutant-general, and Colonel Murray, quarter-master-general, were also forward in affording the most flattering testimonials of their esteem; and this generous youth had the satisfaction to perceive, that although afflicted with a wound which eventually cost him his life, the noble spirit developed at so early a stage of his existence was not without its reward in the approval of men whose military rank and character lent additional weight to their individual approbation.

The appearance of the American prisoners captured at Frenchtown was miserable to the last degree. They had the air of men to whom cleanliness was a virtue unknown, and their squalid bodies were covered by habiliments that had evidently undergone every change of season, and were arrived at the last stage of repair. It has already been remarked that it was the depth of winter; but scarcely an individual was in possession of a great coat or cloak, and few of them wore garments of wool of any description. They still retained their summer dress, consisting of cotton stuff of various colors, shaped into frocks, and descending to the knee; their trowsers were of the same material. They were covered with slouched hats, worn bare by constant use, beneath which their long hair fell matted and uncombed oyer their cheeks: and these, together with the dirty blankets wrapped around their loins to protect them against the inclemency of the season, and fastened by broad leathern belts, into which were thrust axes and knives of an enormous length, gave them an air of wildness and savageness, which in Italy would have caused them to pass for brigands of the Apennines. The only distinction between the garb of the officer and that of the soldier was, that the one, in addition to his sword, carried a short rifle instead of a long one, while a dagger, often curiously worked and of some value, supplied the place of the knife. This description may be considered as applicable to the various hordes of irregular troops sent forth throughout the war from the States of Ohio and Kentucky. The equipment was ever the same, and differing only inasmuch as their opportunities of preserving or renewing it were more or less frequent.

Far from being discouraged by the discomfiture of their armies under Generals Hull and Winchester, the Americans despatched a third and more formidable, under one of their most experienced commanders, General Harrison, who reaching Fort Meigs shortly subsequent to the affair at Frenchtown, directed his attention to the construction of works which rendered his position in some measure impregnable. Determined if possible to thwart the views of the enemy, and give a finishing stroke to his movements in that quarter, General Procter (lately promoted) ordered an expedition to be in readiness to move for the Miami. Accordingly, towards the close of April, a detachment of the 41st, some militia, and 1,5OO Indians, accompanied by a train of battering artillery, and attended by two gunboats, proceeded up that river, and established themselves on the left bank, at the distance of a mile from the site selected for our batteries. The season was unusually wet, yet, in defiance of every obstacle, they were erected the same night in front of the American fortress, and the guns transported along a road in which the axle-trees of the carriages were frequently buried in mud. Among other battering pieces, were two 24-pounders, in the transportation of which 200 men with several oxen, were employed from nine o'clock at night until daybreak in the morning. At length every preparation having been made, a shot from one of the gun-boats was the signal for their opening, and early on the morning of the 1st of May, a heavy fire was commenced, and continued for four days without intermission, during which period everyone of the enemy's batteries, within our range, was silenced and dismantled. The fire of the 24-pounder battery was principally directed against the powder magazine, which the besieged were busily occupied in covering and protecting from our hot shot. It was impossible to have artillery better served; every shot that was fired sank into the roof of the magazine, scattering the earth to a considerable distance, and burying many of the workmen in its bed, from whence we could distinctly perceive the survivors dragging forth the bodies of their slaughtered comrades. Meanwhile the flank companies of the 41st, with a few Indians, had been detached to the opposite shore, within a few hundred yards of the enemy's works, and had constructed a battery, from which a galling cross-fire was maintained. Dismayed at the success of our operations, General Harrison, already apprized before our arrival of the approach of a reinforcement of 1,500 men, then descending the Miami under General Clay, contrived to despatch a courier on the evening of the 4th, with an order for that officer to land immediately, and possess himself of our batteries on the left bank, while he (General Harrison) sallied forth to carry those on the right. Accordingly, at eight o'clock on the morning of the 5th, General Clay pushed forward the whole of his force, and meeting with no opposition at the batteries, which were entirely unsupported, proceeded to spike the guns in conformity with his instructions; but elated with his success, and disobeying the positive order of his chief, which was to retire the instant his object was effected, he continued to occupy the position. In the meantime the flying artillerymen had given the alarm, and three companies of the 41st, several of militia, and a body of Indians, the latter under their celebrated chieftain Tecumseh, were ordered to move on the instant, and repossess themselves of the works. The rain, which had commenced early in the morning, continued to fall with violence, and the road, as has already been described, was knee-deep with mud, yet the men advanced to the assault with the utmost alacrity and determination. The enemy on our approach had sheltered themselves behind the batteries, affording them every facility of defence, yet they were driven at the point of the bayonet from each in succession, until eventually not a man was left in the plain. Flying to the woods, the murderous fire of the Indians drove them back upon their pursuers, so that they had no possibility of escape. A vast number were killed, and independently of the prisoners taken by the Indians, 450, with their second in command, fell into our hands. Every man of the detachment acquitted himself on this occasion to the entire satisfaction of his superiors. Among the most conspicuous for gallantry was Major Chambers of the 41st, acting deputy quarter quarter-master-general to the division. Supported merely by four or five followers, this meritorious officer advanced under a shower of balls from the enemy, and carried one of the batteries sword in hand. A private of the same regiment being opposed in an isolated situation to three Americans, contrived to disarm and render them his prisoners. On joining his company towards the close of the affair, he excited much mirth among his comrades, in consequence of the singular manner in which he appeared, sweating beneath the weight of arms he had secured as trophies of his victory, and driving his captives before him with an air of indifference and carelessness which contrasted admirably with the occasion. Of the whole of the division under General Clay, scarcely 200 men effected their escape. Among the fugitives was that officer himself. The sortie made by General Harrison at the head of the principal part of the garrison had a different result. The detachment supporting the battery already described were driven from their position and two officers, Lieutenants McIntyre and Hailes, and thirty men were made prisoners. Meanwhile, it having been discovered that the guns on the left bank, owing to some error on the part of the enemy, had been spiked with the ramrods of their muskets, instead of the usual instruments, they were speedily rendered serviceable, and the fire from the batteries was renewed. At this moment a white flag was observed waving on the ramparts of the fort, and the courage and perseverance of the troops appeared at length as if about to be crowned by the surrender of a fortress, the siege of which had cost them so much trouble and privation. Such, however, was far from being the intention of General Harrison. Availing himself of the cessation of hostilities which necessarily ensued, he caused the officers and men just captured to be sent across the river for the purpose of being exchanged; but this was only a feint for the accomplishment of a more important object. Drawing up his whole force, both of cavalry and infantry, on the plain beneath the fortress, he caused such of the boats of General Clay's division as were laden with ammunition, of which the garrison stood much in need, to be dropped under the works, and the stores to be immediately disembarked. All this took place during the period occupied in the exchange of prisoners. The remaining boats containing the baggage and private stores of the division, fell into the hands of the Indians, still engaged in the pursuit of the fugitives, and the plunder they acquired was immense. General Harrison, having secured his stores, and received the officers and men exchanged for his captives, withdrew into the garrison, and the bombardment was recommenced.

The victory obtained at the Miami was such as to reflect credit on every branch of the service; but the satisfaction arising from the conviction was deeply embittered by an act of cruelty, which, as the writer of an impartial memoir, it becomes my painful duty to record. In the heat of the action a strong corps of the enemy, who had thrown down their arms, and surrendered themselves prisoners of war, were immediately despatched, under an escort of fifty men, for the purpose of being embarked in the gun-boats, where it was presumed they would be safe from the attacks of the Indians. This measure, however, although dictated by the purest humanity, and apparently offering the most probable means of security, proved one of fatal import to several of the prisoners. On reaching our encampment, then entirely deserted by the troops, they were met by a band of cowardly and treacherous Indians, who had borne no share in the action, yet who now, guided by the savage instinct of their nature, approached the column, and, selecting their victims, commenced the work of blood. In vain did the harassed and indignant escort attempt to save them from the fury of their destroyers; the phrenzy of these wretches knew no bounds, and an old and excellent soldier of the name of Russell, of the 41st, was shot through the heart while endeavoring to wrest a victim from the grasp of his murderer. Forty of these unhappy men had already fallen beneath the steel of the infuriated party, when Tecumseh, apprized of what was doing, rode up at full speed, and raising his tomahawk, threatened to destroy the first man who resisted his injunction to desist. Even on those lawless people, to whom the language of coercion had hitherto been unknown, the threats and tone of the exasperated chieftain produced an instantaneous effect, and they retired at once humiliated and confounded. Never did Tecumseh shine more truly himself than on this occasion; and nought of the savage could be distinguished save the color and the garb. EYer merciful and magnanimous as he was ardent and courageous, the voice of the supplicant seldom reached him in vain; and although war was his idol, the element in which he lived, his heart was formed to glow with all the nobler and more generous impulses of the warrior; nor was his high character less esteemed by ourselves than reverenced by the various tribes over which, in his quality of brother to the Prophet, he invariably presided. In any other country, and governing any other men, Tecumseh would have been a hero; at the head of this uncivilized and untractable people he was a savage; but a savage such as Civilization herself might not blush to acknowledge for her child. Constantly opposed to the encroachments of the Americans for a series of years previous to their rupture with England, he had combatted their armies on the banks of the Wabash with success, and given their leaders proofs of a skill and judgment in defence of his native soil, which would not have disgraced the earlier stages of military science in Europe. General Harrison himself, a commander with whom he had often disputed the palm of victory, with the generous candor of the soldier, subsequently ascribed to him virtues as a man, and abilities as a warrior, commanding at once the attention and admiration of his enemies.

The survivors of this melancholy catastrophe were immediately conveyed on board the gunboats moored in the river; and every precaution having been taken to prevent a renewal of the scene, the escorting party proceeded to the interment of the victims, to whom the rites of sepulture were afforded even before those of our own men who had fallen in the action. Colonel Dudley, second in command of General Clay's division, was among the number of the slain.

On the evening of the second day after this event, I accompanied Major Muir of the 41st, in a ramble throughout the encampment of the Indians, distant a few hundred yards from our own. The spectacle there offered to our view was at once of the most ludicrous and revolting nature. In various directions were lying the trunks and boxes taken in the boats of Gen. Clay's division, and the plunderers were busily occupied in displaying their riches, carefully examining each article, and attempting to divine its use. Several were decked out in the uniforms of the officers; and although embarrassed to the last degree in their movements, and dragging with difficulty the heavy military boots with which their legs were for the first time covered, strutted forth much to the admiration of their less fortunate comrades. Some were habited in plain clothes; others had their bodies clad in clean white shirts, contrasting in no ordinary manner, with the swarthiness of their skins; all wore some article of decoration, and their tents were ornamented with saddles, bridles, rifles, daggers, swords, and pistols, many of which were handsomely mounted and of curious workmanship. Such was the ridiculous part of the picture; but mingled with these, and in various directions, were to be seen the scalps of the slain drying in the sun, stained on the fleshy side with vermilion dyes, and dangling in the air, as they hung suspended from the poles to which they were attached; together with hoops of various sizes, on which were stretched portions of human skin taken from various parts of the body, principally the hand and foot, and yet covered with the nails of those parts; while, scattered along the ground, were visible the members from which they had been separated, and serving as nutriment to the wolf-dogs by which the Indians were accompanied. As we continued to advance into the heart of the encampment, a scene of a more disgusting nature arrested our attention. Stopping at the entrance of a tent occupied by a part of the Minoumini tribe, already spoken of, we observed them seated round a large fire, over which was suspended a kettle containing their meal. Each warrior had a piece of string hanging over the edge of the vessel, and to this was suspended a food, which, it will be presumed we heard not without loathing, consisted of part of an American. Any expression of our feelings, as we declined the invitation they gave us to join in their repast, would have been resented by the Indians without much ceremony. We had, therefore, the prudence to excuse ourselves under the plea we had already taken our food, and we hastened to remove from the contemplation of a sight so revolting to humanity. This was the only instance in which the natives ever appeared to us in the character of Anthropophagi, and the obloquy must in justice fall on this tribe alone. They were the most barbarous of the whole Indian race; and no example can be adduced of a similar disposition being manifested by any one other tribe during the course of our struggle with America.

Since the affair of the 5th the enemy continued to keep themselves shut up within their works, and the bombardment, although followed up with vigour, had effected no practicable breach. From the report made by the officers captured during the sortie from the fort, it appeared that, with a perseverance and toil peculiar to themselves, the Americans had constructed subterranean passages to protect them from the annoyance of our shells, which sinking into beds of clay, softened by the incessant rains that had fallen, instead of exploding, were immediately extinguished. Impatient of longer privation, and anxious to return to their families and occupations, numbers of the militia withdrew themselves in small bodies, and under cover of night: while the majority of the Indians, enriched by plunder, and languishing under the tediousness of a mode of warfare so different from their own, with less ceremony and caution, left us to prosecute the siege as we could. Tecumseh at the head of his own tribe (the Shawnees) and a few others, in all amounting to about four hundred warriors, continued to remain. The troops also were worn down by constant fatigue, for here, as in every other expedition undertaken against the enemy, few even of the officers had tents to shield them from the weather. A few pieces of bark torn from the trees, and covering the skeleton of a hut, was their only habitation, and they were merely separated from the damp earth by a few scattered leaves, on which was generally spread a great coat or blanket by the men, and a cloak by the officers. Hence frequently arose dysentery, ague, and the various other ills to which an army, encamped in a wet and unhealthy position is inevitably subject; and fortunate was he who possessed the skin of the bear or the buffalo, on which he could repose his wearied limbs after a period of suffering and privation, which those who have never served in the wilds of America can with difficulty comprehend. Such was the position of the contending parties towards the middle of May, when General Procter, despairing to effect the reduction of the fort, caused preparations to be made for raising the siege. Accordingly the gun-boats ascended the river, and anchored under the batteries, the guns of which were conveyed on board under a heavy fire from the enemy. The whole being secured, the expedition returned to Amherstburg, the Americans remaining tranquil within their works, and suffering us to depart unmolested.

No. III

Late in July, another expedition, consisting of a part of the 41st and several hundred Indians, accompanied by a few pieces of light artillery, was undertaken against the enemy's fortress on the Miami. Landing on the right side of the river, a small battery of six-pounders was erected on the site of that previously destroyed by General Harrison and rather with a view of decoying the enemy from his stronghold than with ay idea of making a serious impression on his works. After having waited several days in the vain expectation of being attacked, General Procter, to whom information had been conveyed that a supply of provisions was on its route for, and daily expected by the garrison, availing himself of a rainy misty day when the view could not be extended beyond a few hundred yards, caused a heavy fire of musquetry to be kept up by the troops and Indians, posted along the skirt of the wood adjoining the fort, for the purpose of inducing the enemy to believe their convoy was attacked. This stratagem, however, failed to produce the effect desired; the expedition was re-embarked, and its direction changed to Sandusky, a hostile fortress built on the river of than name, emptying itself into Lake Erie at a distance of some leagues, and in a south-western course from the mouth of the Miami.

During the short period that we were employed before Fort Meigs, a young Indian of the Sawkie tribe fell victim to his utter ignorance of the use or effect of shells. Being out with a reconnoitering party of his countrymen among whom a few bombs were thrown from the garrison, he perceived one at some little distance with the fuse still burning. Struck by the novelty of the sight, the young warrior ran up to the spot, and was in the act of touching the shell with his fingers when it exploded, tearing out his bowels, and mangling his limbs in a frightful manner. The fierce wild air of the warriors, whose countenances spoke the desire they entertained of revenging his death, the originality of their costume, contrasting with that of the officers present at the ceremony, and the sombre silence which reigned throughout the group, heightened in effect by a deep gloom of the forest in which they were assembled, composed a singular and romantic picture, in which melancholy grandeur and imposing savageness shone principally conspicuous.

The expedition having reached the Sandusky river early on the 1st of August, a landing was effected on the same day, and within range of the enemy's guns, several ineffectual discharges from which passed over us, as we traversed a plain several hundred yards in extent in order to gain the wood, on the skirt of which it was intended to plant the batteries. These being immediately erected, at daybreak on the following morning our fire was opened, and continued until three 0' clock in the afternoon of the 2nd, when, it being evident that no breach could be effected on the stockade work, General Procter resolved to attempt it by assault. Accordingly at four o'clock the troops divided into three columns of about 120 men each, were put in motion, and advancing through the plain, in double quick time, were suffered to approach within fifty yards, before they were met by the destructive fire of the enemy. The strong line of picketing, constituting their defence, was surrounded by a ditch flanked by batteries, and beyond the ditch was a deep ravine covered with brushwood, and more or less approximate to the place, according to its windings. Far from being checked by the severe fire of the Americans, the divisions redoubled their exertions, and vying with each other to take the lead, dashed down the ravine, and clambering up the opposite steep, were soon beneath the walls of the fort. Not a fascine, however, had been provided; and although axes had been distributed among a body of men selected for the purpose, they were so blunted by constant use, that it would have been the work of hours to cut through the double line of pickets, even if an enemy had not been there to interrupt its progress. In defiance of this difficulty, the axe-men leaped without hesitation into the ditch, and attempted to acquit themselves of their duty; but they were speedily swept away by the guns from the batteries, charged with musket balls and slugs and directed with fatal precision. The troops had established themselves on the edge of the ditch, but it was impossible to scale without the aid of ladders or fascines; and within a few paces of the enemy only, they saw their comrades fall on every hand with no hope of avenging their deaths, The second division had only two officers attached to it. Brevet Lieutenant-Colonel Short, of the 4lst, was killed while descending the ravine at the head of his column, when, the command devolving on Lieutenant Gordon of the same regiment, that officer encouraging his men, and calling on them to follow his example, was one of the first in the ditch, and was in the act of cutting the picketing with his sabre, when a ball, fired from a wall-piece, struck him in the breast. Although dangerously wounded, he refused to abandon his post, and continued to animate his men by his example, until a second ball, fired from the same piece, and lodging in his brain, left the division without an officer. The action had continued nearly two hours without producing the slightest impression on the enemy, when the bugles sounded the "cease-firing," and the men were ordered to lie flat on the ground on the edge of the ravine. The first division were so near the enemy, that they could distinctly hear the various orders given in the fort, and the faint voices of the wounded and dying in the ditch, calling out for water, which the enemy had the humanity to lower to them on the instant. After continuing in this position until nine o'clock, the columns received an order to effect their retreat in silence, which was done accordingly, the enemy merely firing a few volleys of musketry, which produced no material effect. The troops being reimbarked the same night, the expedition descended the river, and returned to Amherstburg. Our loss in this affair was severe: that of the 1st division alone, consisting chiefly of the light company of the 41st, which had attacked the enemy at the strongest point, and under his very works, was five and thirty men.

During the assault, no assistance whatever was afforded by the Indians, who, unaccustomed to this mode of warfare, contented themselves with remaining quiet spectators of the scene. The" devoted men" alone, to whom I have before alluded, followed close in the rear of one of the columns, but they had not long witnessed the effect of the enemy's fire on the divisions, when they retreated to the wood with a precipitation, that with any other people, would be attributed to cowardice, but with the natives it could only be considered as the effect of habit. They expressed much astonishment at the coolness and intrepidity with which the men supported the fire of the enemy, without returning it until arrived at the edge of the ditch; and concluded by saying that they had ever hitherto deemed themselves the bravest nation in the world, but were now willing to concede that distinction to the warriors of their Great Father.

The garrison of Sandusky when attacked, consisted of a force inferior in number to that of the assailing columns, and was commanded by Major Croghan of the line, a promising officer, only nineteen years of age. The gallant defence made by him on this occasion met with the highest encomiums from his countrymen, and he was immediately promoted to the rank of lieutenant-colonel; neither was his conduct without its reward in the approbation of a sex, whose favour and encouragement seldom fail to act as incentives to the acquisition of military fame. The ladies of Ohio (the State in which Colonel Croghan was born) subscribed a considerable sum, with which a handsome sword was purchased and presented by themselves. It is with peculiar satisfaction that I find myself enabled to record an act of courtesy on the part of this gentleman, not unworthy of the days of chivalry. An officer having been despatched to Sandusky with a flag, some days subsequent to the assault, in order to obtain an exchange of the prisoners, who were chiefly wounded, was received with much politeness by the commandant, who at the moment of departure drew from his secretary a pair of pistols, which had been lost in the brushwood of the ravine during our retreat at night. Presuming from the workmanship and style, that they might be, what in fact they actually were, old family arms, and naturally imagining that their loss must be regretted by their possessor, he begged the officer in question to take charge of, and present them to the individual to whom they belonged. It is unnecessary to add that they were gratefully received. [They were my own, and had been lent to the gallant Lieutenant Gordon.]

The period was now fast approaching when the fruits of so much toil and privation were to be wrested from our grasp, and the extensive line of territory, both original and acquired, so gallantly defended by a single regiment against the repeated invasions of the enemy during a period of fifteen months, was to fall beneath the efforts of numerical strength. Since the capture of Detroit, the Americans had been indefatigable in their exertions to establish a superiority of naval force, on which, they well knew, depended the ultimate success of their arms. Buffalo was the harbor selected for the construction of their flotilla, which, under the hands of numerous workmen, soon presented a formidable appearance, and was deemed more than sufficient to ensure their ascendancy on the lake. Manned by experienced seamen taken from several frigates then blockaded in their sea-ports, and commanded by able and intelligent officers, these vessels put forth towards the close of August, and continued cruising off the harbor of Amherstburg, in which our fleet lay awaiting the completion of the Detroit, a vessel of twenty guns then on the stocks, and the arrival of seamen long promised and vainly expected from Lake Ontario. Captain Barclay had arrived some time previous to take the command, and with him several officers and forty men: but notwithstanding every remonstrance on the subject made by the commanding officer of the division, no further assistance was afforded. The remaining part of the crews were provincial sailors, willing and anxious, it is true, to do their duty, but without that perfection and experience in their profession, which are so indispensably necessary to the insurance of success in a combat at sea. In defiance of this disadvantage, the enemy had no sooner made his appearance, than the Detroit was launched in her rough and unfinished state, and armed, in default of other guns, with long battering pieces taken from the ramparts. Every calibre was employed—sixes, nines, twelves, eighteens and even the two twenty-four pounders which had been so successfully used at the Miami. The early part of September was employed in getting in her masts and rigging, and in a few days the fleet was ready to sail. Our position at this period had become exceedingly critical. The want of provisions began to be seriously felt, and the ultimate possession of the garrison depended wholly on the result of the naval conflict, for which both parties were preparing. In the event of the enemy being successful, not only must we be open to the incursions of the large forces, then collected in several quarters, and ready to overwhelm us at the moment that the command of the lake would afford them facility of movement, but the means of obtaining supplies from Fort Erie must be entirely cut off. The quantity of provisions already consumed had been enormous; for independently of the wanton destruction of cattle by the Indians, who often shot or stabbed them merely to possess themselves of the horns, in which they secured their powder, leaving the carcasses to putrefy in the sun, ten thousand rations were daily issued to the warriors and their families: the latter apparently increasing in numbers, as our means of supplying them became more contracted.

Such was the situation of the garrison, reduced in its regular force to a handful of men, by the losses sustained in the various engagements herein detailed, when Captain Barclay, who had hoisted his flag on board the Detroit, made the signal, early in the morning of the 9th, to weigh anchor and bear across the lake. The little fleet, consisting of six sail, had not long left the port before they were perceived by the enemy, then lying among a cluster of islands at some leagues distance, who immediately bore up under a light side-wind, favorable at that moment to the approach of the two squadrons. At one o'clock the engagement commenced. The Detroit leading into action, was opposed to the Lawrence, mounting eighteen thirty-two pounders, and commanded by the American Commodore; and such was the effect of the long guns, that the latter vessel was soon compelled to strike her flag, having only eighteen serviceable men left. The Detroit and Queen Charlotte had, however, suffered severely in their sails and rigging from the fire of the enemy's gunboats; and not only everyone of their boats had been so severely wounded as to render it impossible to take possession of the prize; but the united and unceasing exertions of their crews could not prevent them from running foul of each other. Availing himself of this unfortunate accident, Commodore Perry, who had shifted his flag to the Niagara, a vessel of equal force with the Lawrence, bore up and discharged his broadside with murderous effect. Waring immediately, a second and equally destructive followed, and in this manner was the action continued, rendering resistance almost hopeless. The other smaller vessels, already warmly engaged, could afford no aid, and the guns of the unfortunate wrecks were at length nearly all unserviceable,-those at least of the only batteries which could be brought to bear upon the enemy. Almost every officer had been compelled to leave the deck, and the helplessness of the crews could only be exceeded by their despair, when after two hours and a half of incessant cannonading, the British flag was replaced by the Eagles of America.

The anxiety with which the issue of the combat was awaited at Amherstburg, where the firing was distinctly heard, may easily be conceived. From the heights overhanging the lake, and nearly opposite to the islands, the first encounter of the fleets was clearly observed, but the thick columns of smoke in which they were speedily enveloped, precluded all possibility of following the progress of the contest; nor was it until the thunder of the artillery had been some time discontinued, that the clouds of vapour gradually dispelling, presented the melancholy picture of our vessels, several of them crippled and dismasted, following in the track of the American fleet, then directing its course towards the bay of Sandusky.

In this affair, so unfavorable in its result to our already precarious cause, the enemy had the most decided advantage, not only in respect to superiority of seamen, but in number of ships, and in weight of metal. Their fleet consisted of nine sail, of which the two principal, the Lawrence and Niagara, mounted eighteen thirty-two pounders. Four others were armed with a long gun of the same calibre, and, keeping aloof during the action, were enabled by the calm state of the lake to do much execution among our principal vessels, which were completely raked by their destructive fire. the principal vessels composing Captain Barclays' force were—the Detroit, twenty guns; Queen Charlotte, twenty guns; Lady Prevost, twelve guns; General Hunter, six guns; and two small craft, one of which mounted a mortar, the other a long eighteen-pounder; and the whole weight of the metal did not amount to 1100 pounds: while that of the enemy, exclusive of the three remaining vessels of their flotilla each mounting several guns, was 1,280: and when it is taken into consideration that the accident which occurred early in the engagement to the two principal ships, prevented all possibility of bringing a second broadside to bear, while the enemy, on the contrary, were enabled to avail themselves of their whole metal, the disproportion will appear even more enormous. Notwithstanding the disparity of force, however, a different result might have been expected, had the unceasing applications made for sailors been attended to by the naval commander on Lake Ontario, to whose unwillingness to part with men, who might very well have been spared for the occasion, must be attributed the sacrifice of the gallant Barclay and his fleet, and eventually that of the Right Division. The necessity of haying regular and experienced seamen was never more cruelly exemplified than on the present occasion; since, in all probability, had they been present, the accident which left the Detroit and Queen Charlotte entirely at the mercy of the enemy, would either have been prevented, or remedied in time. All that courage and perseverance could effect was done: but against the decrees of destiny who may successfully oppose himself? Captain Barclay, who had already lost one limb while fighting the battles of his country, was so severely wounded in his only remaining arm as to be compelled to leave the deck early in the action. Captain Finnis, commanding the Queen Charlotte, was killed by a round shot soon afterwards, and the same ball carried off Lieutenant Garden, a promising young officer of the Newfoundland Regiment, mingling the blood of the one and the brains of the other, on the bulwark, in one melancholy and undistinguishable mass. I had subsequently an opportunity of witnessing the devastation of this sanguinary day. The decks were literally filled with the wounded; and such was the crippled state of the Detroit, that not a mast was left standing: almost all the guns were dismounted, and it was impossible to place a hand on that side which had been exposed to the enemy's fire, without covering part of a wound, either from grape, canister, or round shot.

With the loss of our fleet vanished every hope of maintaining our positions against the enemy, who, already assembled in the neighborhood of Forts Sandusky and Meigs, to the number of ten thousand men, only awaited the result of the action to decide on their future movements. A vast number of boats had been collected for the purpose of transporting them across the lake, under cover of their squadron, whose recent Success leaving them undisputed masters of that element, necessarily precluded all probability of effectual opposition. A council was accordingly assembled, and the various chieftains summoned to attend. After a brief exposition of the defenceless state of the garrison. the almost utter impossibility of preventing the landing of the enemy, and the alarming destitution into which the magazines of provision had fallen, General Procter proposed that the forts of Detroit and Amherstburg, together with the various public buildings, should be destroyed, and that the troops and Indians should retire on the Centre Division at Niagara. This proposal was met by the chieftains with divided sentiments; but Tecumseh, whose gallant and impetuous spirit could ill brook he idea of retiring before his enemies, had no sooner heard the conclusion, than he arose, and, in a speech of much length, and accompanied by powerful energy and gesticulation, protested against the infamy of abandoning the position without first using every exertion for its defence. He addressed the commanding officer in the severest terms; accused him of cowardice; and after having compared his conduct with that of Captain Barclay, whose noble defence had inspired him with an enthusiasm surpassed only by the regret he entertained at his failure, concluded by declaring it to be his fixed determination to remain with his warriors and defend the place himself. The effect of his speech was instantaneous. No sooner had the last words died away upon his lips, than the various chieftains started up to a man, and brandishing their tomahawks in the most menacing manner, vociferated their approbation of his sentiments. The scene altogether was of the most imposing character. The council-room was a large, lofty building, the vaulted roof of which echoed back the wild yell of the Indians; while the threatening attitude and diversified costume of these latter formed a striking contrast with the calm demeanor and military garb of the officers grouped around the walls. The most prominent feature in the picture, however, was Tecumseh. Habited in a close leather dress, his athletic proportions were admirably delineated, while a large plume of white ostrich feathers, by which he was generally distinguished, overshadowing his brow, and contrasting with the darkness of his complexion and the brilliancy of his black and piercing eye, gave a singularly wild and terrific expression to his features. It was evident that he could be terrible. Tranquillity being at length restored, General Procter, through the medium of his interpreters, entered into a more detailed account of the motives by which he was influenced, and finally succeeded in prevailing on the warrior to assent to a second proposal, which was to retire on the Moravian village, distant nearly halfway between Amherstburg and the outposts of the Centre Division, and there await the approach of the enemy.

It having been resolved to move without loss of time, the troops were immediately employed in razing the fortifications, and committing such stores as it was found impossible to remove to the flames, kindled in the various public buildings; and the ports of Detroit and Amherstburg for some days previous to our departure presented a scene of cruel desolation. At length, the baggage waggons and boats having been sent in advance, the troops of the latter garrison commenced their march early in the last week of September, and being joined by those of Detroit, proceeded up the mouth of the Thames, a river navigable for small craft, and separated from that of Detroit by the Lake St. Clair, into which it empties itself. Our movements were extremely dilatory; and although the bridge near Amherstburg, already described in the early part of this narrative, had been destroyed by our rear-guard, it was speedily repaired by the American general who, on the third day after our departure from Amherstburg, crossed the lake in boats; and hastening to overtake us with a corps of five thousand men, was within a few leagues at the moment we approached the position where it was originally intended the little army should intrench itself.

The Moravian village, situated in a small plain, offered every facility of defence, being bounded on one flank by a thick wood, highly favourable to the operations of the Indians, and on the other, by the river Thames, while immediately in front, a deep ravine, covered with brushwood, and commanded by our guns, presented an obstacle peculiarly unfavorable to the passage of cavalry, of which, we were sufficiently informed, a large portion of the advancing columns consisted. Yet, notwithstanding the excellence of the position, from some singularly selfish motive, the project was entirely abandoned. On the evening of the 4th, the enemy had captured our boats and, with them, the guard by which they were accompanied. On the 5th, at one o'clock in the afternoon, we were within two miles of the Moravian village, but in defiance of that repeated experience which should have taught us the hopelessness of combating a concealed enemy, the troops were ordered to defile into the heart of a wood, not very close it is true, yet through the interstices of which it was impossible for the view to extend itself beyond a distance of twenty paces, much less to discover objects bearing so close a resemblance to the bark and foliage of the trees and bushes as the costume of the Americans; whereas, on the contrary, the glaring red of the troops formed a point of relief on which the eye could not fail to dwell. In this position we continued to remain during two hours, our left wing extending to the road, in which a solitary six pounder was posted, and the right flanked by the Indians to the number of I,OOO under Tecumseh; when the bugles of the enemy sounding at length to the attack, the engagement commenced. The result of an affair against a body of such numerical superiority, and under such circumstances, may easily be anticipated. Closely pressed on every hand, and principally by a strong corps of mounted riflemen, the troops were finally compelled to give way, and completely hemmed in by their assailants, had no other alternative than to lay down their arms-fifty men only, with a single officer of the regiment, Lieut. Bullock of the 41st, contriving to effect their escape through the wood. General Procter, mounted on an excellent courser, and accompanied by his personal staff, sought safety in flight at the very commencement of the action, and being pursued for some hours by a detachment of cavalry, was in imminent danger of falling into their hands. Being subsequently tried for his conduct in this affair, on charges preferred by Lieutenant-colonel Warburton, inspecting field-officer, and Brevet-Major Chambers, acting deputy quarter-master general, he was suspended from rank and pay for six months.

In this affair, I had an opportunity of witnessing the cruel dexterity and despatch with which the Indians use the tomahawk and scalping knife. A Kentucky rifleman, who had been dismounted within a few yards of the spot where I stood, was fired at by three warriors of the Delaware tribe. The unfortunate man received their several balls in his body, yet, although faint from loss of blood, he made every exertion to save himself. The foremost of his pursuers was a tall powerful man. When arrived within twelve or fifteen paces of his victim, uncovered in his flight, he threw his tomahawk, and with such force and precision, that it immediately opened the skull, and extended him motionless on the earth. Laying down his rifle, he drew forth his knife, and after having removed the hatchet from the brain, proceeded to make a circular incision throughout the scalp. This done, he grasped the bloody instrument between his teeth, and placing his knees on the back of his victim, while at the same time he fastened his fingers in the hair, the scalp was torn off without much apparent difficulty and thrust, still bleeding, into his bosom. The warrior then arose, and after having wiped his knife on the clothes of the unhappy man, returned it to its sheath, grasping at the same time the arms he had abandoned, and hastening to rejoin his comrades. All this was the work of a minute.

The severest loss we sustained was that of the gallant and unfortunate Tecumseh. In the early part of the action, he had been personally opposed to Colonel Johnson, commanding the American riflemen, and having severely wounded that officer with a ball from his rifle, was in the act of springing upon him with his tomahawk, when his adversary drew a pistol from his belt, and shot him dead on the spot. No sooner had he fallen, than a party of Americans, seizing his lifeless body, proceeded to strip him of his skin, which they subsequently converted into razor straps! thus testifying, in their anxiety to obtain this species of trophy, the dread they entertained of the warlike chieftain, while living, and the degree of importance they attached to his death. When the account of his fate was conveyed to the officers of the division, the most lively regret was manifested by each; and for some time, the bitter impressions arising from a sense of captivity, were absorbed in the melancholy inspired by his fall. It is not less an eulogy to the memory of the noble-minded Tecumseh, than a justice due to General Harrison to add that that officer was the first to deplore his death; and the sentiments he expressed when the circumstance and manner of his fall were made known, were such as to reflect credit on himself, both as a man, a gentleman, a Christian, and a soldier.

The advantage obtained by the enemy was subsequently promulgated in pompous terms, in a general order issued by Governor Selby, under whose immediate command the American riflemen were placed. A copy of this unique production afterwards fell into the hands of Lieutenant Cochrane of the 41st, by whom it is, I believe, still preserved as a specimen of Kentuckian literature and Kentuckian modesty. The style was evidently an attempted imitation of the Bulletins of the Grand Army of Napoleon; and a person unacquainted with the event to which it owed its being, would have been tempted to imagine the achievement of the Army of Ohio and Kentucky little inferior to those of the victors of Austerlitz. Among other comparisons, all of singular and equally appropriate character, was that of an officer of little note, killed in the engagement, with Dessaix at the battle of Marengo! To cite its absurdities, however, would be to cite the despatch; and to give that its due weight the orthography and style are indispensably necessary. Governor Selby was a stout vulgar-looking man, resembling rather, in air and manner, one of the drovers by which the army was accompanied, than the chief magistrate of a province. To the custody of this invincible and his legions (as they were classically termed) were the prisoners delivered over by General Harrison, for the purpose of being conducted into the heart of the American wilderness; and on the morning of 7th we commenced our march, traversing at length as captives, and for the last time, that territory we had so long struggled to secure from the grasp of the invader.

The detail of our imprisonment, the seclusion of the officers as hostages, and the various indignities we were compelled to endure from a vindictive and infuriated people, to whom the bare idea of any thing British was a source of detestation, will form the second part of this memoir.

No. IV

Immediately after our capture, and as we passed along the American line, the whole of their Indian force, consisting of about a hundred men, and the first we had hitherto beheld in the enemy's ranks, suddenly appeared before us. With the knowledge we possessed of the Indian character, their utter disregard of all authority, and the almost impossibility of restraining their barbarous usages, there were few of the officers who did not expect to experience in themselves a repetition of those atrocities of which they had more than once been pained and unwilling spectators. Much to our surprise, however, instead of warriors with eyes expressing a thirst of blood, and hands upraised to wield the murderous tomahawk, we beheld a body of men on whose speaking features might be traced the deepest sympathy and commiseration for our fate. Several who had been at Amherstburg previous to the war, and gad gad daily opportunities at that period of seeing both officers and men, smiled and nodded their heads in token of recognition as we passed, and the general conduct of the whole, as they stood calmly leaning on their rifles, was confirmatory of the fact long since conveyed to us, that the services of these men, under the American banners, were entirely compulsory; they having been reduced to the necessity of preserving the lives of their women and children, detained as hostages in the United States, by an appearance of devotedness to the cause of a people for whom the natives have ever entertained the most rooted and unqualified aversion. Notwithstanding this fact, however, it would be an injustice to the character of General Harrison not to state that every precaution had been taken by himself, and that any attempt at the wanton destruction of prisoners would have been visited by him in the severest manner, so that had the Indians even evinced a hostile bearing towards us, the conviction of their being rendered completely subject by their numerical inferiority to the American power, must have had the effect of curbing, if not wholly repressing, their natural ferocity—an advantage, which for the sake of humanity it is to be regretted we never sufficiently possessed, since it will be recollected that the warriors attached to our division were more than trebly superior to us in numbers, and many of them taken from those wild and ungovernable hordes which knew no law but their own will, and held the whites, both friends and foes in the most sovereign contempt.

The officers were received by General Harrison and Commodore Perry, who had volunteered his services on this occasion in the capacity of aid-de-camp to the American commander, with a politeness and cordiality which, while reflecting credit on themselves, proved no less gratifying to their prisoners. Our troops had not tasted food during the day; a circumstance of which General Harrison was no sooner apprised than he caused several bullocks to be instantly killed and distributed. Neither the victors nor the vanquished were in possession of a single tent; and as the evening drew on, enormous fires were kindled in the forest, around the principal of which we remained grouped during the night, squatted like savages on the ground. Large pieces of meat were thrust on pointed sticks, and held before the fire until sufficiently warmed to be eaten without inconvenience, and these, unaccompanied by the luxury either of salt or bread, were devoured with no common appetite, the young Aids-de-camp of the General kindly officiating as cooks, and supplying our wants in succession.

The American bivouac was kept in a state of constant alarm during the night, by repeated slight attacks on the part of the Indians, who, although dispersed in the first instance, were speedily enabled by their familiarity with the woods to reunite in small bodies, and renew their desultory warfare. At a late hour a detachment of horsemen that had been despatched by the governor of Kentucky in pursuit of General Procter, returned in undisguised ill-humour at the ill success attendant on their mission. Mounted on an excellent charger, that officer had fled early in the engagement, and was consequently at the outset much in advance of his pursuers; but encountering numerous obstacles in the baggage-wagons and gun-carriages which obstructed his passage into what is called the Twenty-four Mile Wood, at a distance of five leagues from the scene of the action, he had not made much progress in the deep heavy road by which it is intersected, when the Kentuckians appeared at its skirt. Despairing, however, of eventual success, as their horses had become incapable of much farther exertion, and deeming the fugitive considerably more in advance than he actually was, they here relinquished the pursuit; and after plundering the wagons, returned to the main body of the army. Fortunate was this circumstance for General Procter, since the Kentuckians had sworn his destruction; and General Harrison assured us that, however deeply he might have deprecated ad lamented the act, no quarter would have been given him. Impressed with a false idea that the several cruelties inflicted on their countrymen by the Indians had ever borne the sanction of the officer commanding at Amherstburg, the irregular troops composing the majority of the invading army had resolved on his death; and as they had the tacit, if not avowed sanction of their butcher-like governor and immediate commander, the hero already alluded to, the authority of the general-in-chief would have been utterly disregarded.

Among the number of those whose deaths the Americans were most anxious to avenge, was a Captain Hart, a native of Kentucky, and an universal favourite. This officer had unfortunately perished in the affair of the 22d of January at Frenchtown, but whether during the engagement, or subsequently in cold blood by the Indians, was a question which could not be satisfactorily decided. The Kentuckians obstinately maintained the latter. On retiring from the field with his prisoners, General Procter had been compelled to leave several Americans, too severely wounded to admit of their being transported to Amhersthurg, in one of the block-houses, which had been so gallantly defended, and a small party of militia were left to protect them. These, however, were too feeble to oppose any resistance to the large bands of Indians returning from the 'pursuit and slaughter of the discomfited enemy, who proceeded to fill up the measure of their cruelties by the destruction of these ill-fated men. The block-house was set on fire, and most of those within perished in the flames. Such, the Americans declared, had been the end of Captain Hart; and the vengeance they had vowed to take on him whom they conceived the author of this calamity, was at once summary and severe. Another individual devoted to their wrath, was Captain Elliott of the Essex Militia, a gentleman long resident at Amherstburg, whom they unjustly accused as having been accessary to this melancholy catastrophe; and we subsequently heard his own brother, a captain in the American navy, and the second in command of their fleet in the action of the 10th of September, declare at a public dinner-table, that, in the event of his brother falling into his hands, he would be the first to apply a halter to his neck! Had he or any of his countrymen been aware of the circumstance of my having a pair of boots on my legs at the moment with the name of Captain Hart written at length in the lining, they might have been disposed to render me the same service as one equally implicated in the transaction; and so strong was their feeling in this particular instance, that to have accounted for their being in my possession, by stating the fact of their having been purchased from one of the Indians, into whose hands the whole of the baggage belonging to General Winchester's army had fallen, would not, I am persuaded, have been considered a sufficient plea to prevent the infliction of some personal violence.

During their return to Detroit, the army continued to be harassed by the Indians, who, anxious to avenge the death of their favourite chieftain, hung upon the American rear, and, although incapable of making any serious impression, occasioned them some loss. Wearied with fatigue, and nearly exhausted with hunger, we at length reached the hospitable mansion of Mr. Mackintosh, on the Canadian shore, and nearly opposite to the American fortress. This gentleman, the first in wealth and respectability as a merchant, had some years previous to the war married his eldest daughter to an American residing at Detroit, the son of an officer of rank, much distinguished throughout the revolutionary contest. This connexion naturally served as a guarantee for the preservation of his property; and while we beheld on every hand the most cruel traces of devastation and wonton destruction, effected by hordes of irregulars, even during our short absence, the flourishing fields and rich establishments of Mr. Mackintosh remained unharmed. The hospitality of this gentleman had for a series of years been experienced by the officers successively stationed at Amherstburg, many of whom had been received into his family on the most friendly terms—an intimacy which had recently terminated in the marriage of his third daughter with Lieutenant Troughton, commanding the artillery attached to the right division. Placed in the singular position of having two of his children united to subjects of powers in a state of active hostility, serving on the same theatre, and under his own immediate observation—to have beheld one a prisoner beneath the banners of the other must have excited feelings of a very contradictory and disagreeable nature. This mortification was, however, spared to Mr. Mackintosh, Lieutenant Troughton being one of the few who escaped. His young bride had preceded him some days previous to the affair; and after having in common with the other officers' wives, endured every species of privation and difficulty on the road, finally succeeded in reaching the centre division with the remaining fugitives in safety. With a kindness in no way diminished, either by the change in our position or the presence of several American officers of rank quartered on his house, Mr. Mackintosh received and welcomed us to his table, endeavouring to make up in attention what circumstances and the occasion caused to be deficient in convenience. After having been provided with an abundant repast, we found a large field-bed prepared in the principal drawing-room; and here for the first time since the commencement of our retreat, did we enjoy the luxury of a few hours of undisturbed repose. While seated round the large blazing fire, which threw its cheerful beans along the walls, as if in mockery of the bleak October wind that whistled against the casements, we essayed to divest us of some portion of our apparel. No small difficulty was experienced in the attempt to free our long-imprisoned legs and feet; the latter being much swollen with constant exercise, and identifying as it were with the elastic substance. All were, however, finally successful save myself. Neither art, effort, nor perseverance availed me aught, and Captain Hart's boots, like avenging spirits, clung to my aching limbs with ill-boding pertinacity. Yet of the danger incurred by their possessor, in the event of discovery, I was too well aware, not to employ a final and efficient means. A penknife drawn, though not without some risk, from the extremity of the foot to the top of leg, divided the tenacious leather, and compelled it to yield the guardianship of my feet to a pair of large ammunition-shoes, which I had picked up the day after the action among the scattered remains of our plundered baggage. This point effected, my next precaution was to burn that part of the leather which bore the fatal name, in order that it might not be brought forward at any future period as "damning proof" against those in the neighbourhood of whose dwellings the remaining relics might be found.

On reaching Detroit, we found that the route intended for the march of the prisoners into the state of Ohio was that of Fort Meigs. The officers, having pledged their parole to General Harrison, were suffered to take the advance, mounted on pack-horses provided by the American government. A few only, reserved for the Sandusky route, were embarked in a small vessel of war, and conveyed to Put-in-bay Island, where we had an opportunity of seeing our friends on board the different ships of the squadron. Captain Barclay was still confined to his bed by the severity of his wound, and the number of sufferers scattered throughout the fleet was much greater than we had anticipated. Of the fury with which both parties had maintained the contest there was sufficient evidence in the crippled state of the larger vessels, which still lay with masts, guns, and cordage encumbering their decks, and affording a melancholy proof of the enemy's superiority in weight of metal. On the second morning of our arrival at this island, after having taken on board such of the naval officers as were not prevented by the severity of their wounds from performing the journey, we continued our course for Sandusky Bay. We had nearly made the spot intended for our disembarkation, when one of those dangerous and sudden hurricanes, peculiar to the lakes of Canada during the autumnal months, drove us back under bare poles to the port we had just quitted, and along the sheet of foam with which the broad expanse of water was literally covered. At length we finally separated from our companions in misfortune, and after a few hours' sail were enabled to cast anchor in the bay, where, being immediately landed, we were conducted to the fort of Sandusky,

During our stay at this place we had full leisure for examining not only the defences of the fortress, but the various positions occupied by our troops during the assault; and the result of our observation was, that an attack on a stockade work of this description, without the aid of ladders must inevitably entail discomfiture. The nature of the fortification, and the manner in which the enemy were protected from our fire, may be judged of from the fact of their having had only one man killed in the affair.

That which most excited my own immediate attention was the ground occupied by the left column of attack, consisting chiefly of the light company of the 41st, to which I was then attached, and which having forced their way to the very batteries of the fort had consequently sustained the greatest loss. My escape from the ravine, where we had continued so many hours, was truly providential. When the order for retiring was, in order to deceive the enemy, given in the Indian language, it was immediately explained by several interpreters present with the grenadier column on the right, and conveyed by them in a low voice to the remaining divisions. Covered by the brow of the opposite eminence, they followed the course of the ravine in safety, until they emerged from the defile, at a distance sufficient to admit of their forming unperceived by the enemy. Nearly all the men of the light column, having received the order, had retired with the main body; but those on the extreme left, having been separated from the line by the brushwood and other obstacles they had encountered in the ascent, remained in utter ignorance of what was passing on the right; and such was the caution observed in retiring, that neither the enemy in the fort nor ourselves could distinguish the slightest sound to justify the supposition. It was now half-past nine o'clock. We had continued since half-past five lying extended on the wet ground, where the mud was ankle-deep, and most of the men were chilled with cold, At this moment we heard, though indistinctly, various orders given in the direction of our encampment, and then only did we surmise the fact of the troops having been withdrawn. In this belief we were speedily confirmed, by hearing a command issued in a suppressed tone of voice in the fort, to open the sally-ports. Perceiving that no time was to be lost, I proposed in a whisper, which the rising ground prevented being overheard by the enemy, that we should brave every risk, and attempt our immediate retreat. The men, however, refused to move, until the moon, which was then in the first quarter, and reflecting its beams everywhere but in the bed of the ravine, was set, or should be obscured by some passing cloud. Leaving them to their fate, I therefore prepared to effect my escape alone, and immediately in front of the fortress; but notwithstanding all my caution, I had not advanced many paces, when I stumbled over the dead body of a soldier, who, after having received a mortal wound, had evidently crawled on his hands and knees to rest his bleeding form against a clump of bushes, and had died in that singular position. The noise occasioned by my fall put the enemy once more on the alert; and as the moonbeams reflected on my arms and regimentals, I had no sooner ascended the opposite side of the ravine, than the whole front of the fort was lighted up with their fire. Not an individual, save myself, was exposed to their aim, and the distance did not exceed fifty paces: yet, although the balls whistled round my ears in every direction, and hissed through the long grass with which the plain was covered, I did not sustain the slightest injury, even though a second volley was fired after the interval of half a minute. On reaching the spot where the columns had been originally formed for the assault, I found that my retreat had been well-timed, for the troops were already in motion towards the boats, the guns having been previously embarked. In that which contained my provision-basket, I discovered a few bottles of port wine, which had arrived that very morning from Amherstburg. This was indeed a luxury that I would not at the moment have exchanged for a throne; and so thoroughly exhausted was I with hunger, thirst and fatigue, that placing a bottle to my parched lips, I did not abandon it until the whole of its contents had been emptied at a draught. The effect was instantaneous, and I lay in the bottom of the boat all night enjoying the most delicious moments of repose I recollect ever having experienced, When I awoke at a late hour on the following morning, a mild September sun was glancing its golden rays along the tranquil bosom of Lake Erie, in the centre of which our boats were all assembled, and gliding along its surface with a speed proportioned to the vigorous efforts of the rowers, the men alternately singing and indulging in rude jests, reckless of the comrades whose dying groans had assailed their ears a few hours before, and evidently without care or thought for the future. Every individual of those who had refused to accompany me on that occasion was taken prisoner by the American party despatched through the sally-port.

Some difficulty was experienced at Sandusky in procuring the means of conveyance; at length, however, on the morning of the third day, mounted on miserable pack horses, scarcely able to sustain their own weight, and tottering at every step beneath their additional burden, we commenced our route for Chillicothe, the place selected for our detention. A single officer of infantry composed our escort, and he had been appointed to the service chiefly with a view to protect us from insult, and to procure lodgings and other accommodations on the road. To describe the fatigue and privation which we endured during this tedious journey would require more time and space than it can be necessary to bestow upon this part of the narrative. The rainy season had already set in, and scarcely a single day passed by without our being literally wet to the skin. Our route lay through an inhospitable tract of country, consisting alternately of gloomy forest and extensive savannah, the latter often intersected by streams fed from the distant mountains, and swollen by the unceasing rains. Sometimes a solitary hut, vying in filthiness with the beings by whom it was tenanted, afforded us shelter for the night, but more frequently we found that repose which absolute fatigue and exhaustion ensure to the traveller near the fires we were compelled to kindle in the forest. At length our jaded animals, slipping at every step, and threatening to sink beneath their efforts, brought us to Fort Wayne. Here we were provided with other horses, but of the same miserable description: their backs cruelly galled by the ill-stuffed saddles, and their ribs almost protruding from beneath their hair-divested hides. The appearance of these unfortunate animals was pitiable in the extreme; and few of us, on leaving Fort Wayne, entertained the slightest doubt of their sinking successively beneath us, before our destination could be gained. The rain still continued to fall, and during the latter part of October and the commencement of November we never once beheld the sun. Many of the officers were without great coats, having been plundered of everything, as well by the followers of the division as by the enemy themselves; and, although we each possessed a change of linen, during the whole journey we had no opportunity of having anything washed, so that in a short time we were infested by vermin, which gave the finishing stroke to our calamities. Still we proceeded on our journey, and through a country of the same character with that we had previously traversed. On one occasion we found ourselves stopped by a stream of considerable depth, the bridge over which had been broken down by the torrent. No other alternative remained than to swim our horses across, or run the risk of their breaking their legs in the interstices of the bridge, which had partly sunk beneath the surface of the water. The former course was, after due deliberation, adopted; and lots having been drawn, the first attempt devolved on Lieutenant Stokoe of the Royal Navy.[3] Spurring his horse into the current, this officer with much difficulty reached the opposite bank; but, unable to effect a landing, was thrown from his seat in

---

[3] This gallant officer has since fallen a victim to his enterprising spirit, having perished in Africa while forming one of an expedition destined to explore the source of the Niger.

consequence of the violent struggles made by the animal, and, with one foot fastened in the stirrup, lay for some moments in imminent danger of perishing. At length, after much exertion, he succeeded in disengaging himself, when clambering up the steep, he soon drew his horse after him. This experiment being considered' too dangerous for repetition, we decided on effecting our passage across the bridge; and owing to the caution we observed, no accident occurred to the horses—a circumstance peculiarly fortunate, since we could have found no means of supplying our loss. After several weeks of tedious traveling through this dreary region some few traces of civilization and cultivation were perceptible, and we finally beheld the banks of the Scioto. On the opposite shore of this small river stands the town of Chillicothe; and after having for the last time committed our steeds and persons to the water, in default of a bridge, we found ourselves at the termination of our journey, overcome with lassitude, and in a state which might have caused us to pass for anything rather than British officers. The party which had taken the route of Fort Meigs was already arrived, and with it the troops of the division,

At Chillicothe I was singularly fortunate in meeting with a gentleman who in consideration of some distant branches of my family with whom he was acquainted, exercised the rites of hospitality in my favor to the fullest extent; and it is with peculiar satisfaction that I find myself thus enabled to express my obligations to Henry Brush, Esq. for the uniform attention paid me during the months we were suffered to retain our liberty on parole. No sooner was he apprised of my arrival, than an apartment was prepared and appropriated to my service, a cover daily laid at his table, and his horses declared at my command. In short, no individual in the character of a prisoner of war had ever less reason to inveigh against his destiny. This ray of sunshine was, however, of short duration. Soon after the arrival of the Sandusky party at Chillicothe, the officers captured at the Moravian village were, in consequence of an order from the American government, despatched to Frankfort, the capital of Kentucky, those of the naval party alone being suffered to remain, and, through the influence used by my kind host, my name was included in the list of the latter. At the moment when we began to reconcile ourselves to our situation, and to appreciate the attention paid us by the more respectable inhabitants, an order suddenly arrived for our close imprisonment. This unexpected measure owed its origin to the following circumstance. Among the prisoners taken at the affair in which the lamented General Brock lost his life, twenty-three men, recognized as deserters from the various regiments in Canada, had been sent to England, and subsequently tried and convicted. The execution of the sentence, had, however, been deferred. The American government was no sooner apprized of their impending fate, than, acting on that system of naturalization which, in defiance of every principle of equity, would preclude the hitherto undisputed right of nations to punish their criminal subjects, they caused an equal number of British soldiers to be kept closely confined to answer as hostages for the safety of the convicted deserters. This unjustifiable proceeding was followed by the seclusion of twenty-three commissioned, and an equal number of non-commissioned American officers, and retaliated by them in a similar manner; so that finally nearly all the officers of both parties were deprived of their liberty, and liable at any moment to answer with their lives for the apostasy of three and twenty individuals America should have blushed to claim as subjects of her republic. that the threat of retaliation would have been carried into effect by the government, it is scarcely possible to believe, since, exclusively of the blot of such a proceeding must have imprinted on their character, the disproportion of prisoners was greatly in our favour, as well as in regard to rank as numbers; but we had too much reason to apprehend, from the unqualified hatred manifested towards us by the populace in the states of Ohio and Kentucky, that the will of their rulers would have had little effect in restraining the ebullition of their rage, had the original sentence been carried into execution. Let it not be imagined that this idea arose simply from surmise, or had its being in the vague apprehension of men who, more immediately interested in the result, might be deemed ready to admit the agency of fancy in their impressions of impending evil. Several gentlemen, estimable for their rank and character in these states, warned us during their occasional visits of the fact; and with every opportunity of ascertaining the public feeling, communicated circumstances which left us no reason to infer that their fears for the result should be disregarded. Our sensations in consequence were not, it will be imagined, of the most pleasing or enviable description. The common gaol of the town had been fixed on for our abode, and we were distributed into two small rooms in an upper story, communicating with each other, and containing each ten persons. During the day they were left open, but carefully locked and bolted at night, and sentinels were posted in the corridor into which they opened. The height was upwards of sixty feet from the ground; and through the strong bars with which the windows were furnished, we beheld others pacing to and fro, and exercising their vigilance so far as to direct their attention repeatedly to our rooms. Thus guarded, and unprovided with instruments of any description whatever, we had no hope of effecting an escape; while, to crown our misery, fortune had thrown us into the hands of a gaoler of the most ruffian-like character. On one occasion, in consequence of some trifling misunderstanding with an interpreter who had been confined in the adjoining room—a man remarkable for the mildness and forbearance of his nature,—the wretch inflicted so severe a wound on his head with a ponderous key, as to cause the blood to gush forth with extreme violence. When visited by the officer of the guard, a complaint was preferred by the injured man; but the liberal republican, with true patriotic feeling, justified the act of his countryman, and concluded by threatening a repetition of the punishment.

We had now been some time in this disagreeable situation, when a project was formed which promised to throw a more favorable coloring over our destiny. The whole of the captive division, including the seamen, were confined in a fortified camp, erected for the purpose on the skirt of a wood adjoining one of the suburbs of the town, and were guarded by a considerable detachment of regular infantry. These noble fellows were no sooner apprized of the ignominious fate with which their officers were threatened, than with the generous devotedness characteristic of their respective professions, they deputed two sergeants who had been suffered to communicate with us on subjects relative to the clothing of the men, to express their determination to effect our liberation, or perish in the attempt. Accordingly, the following plan was adopted, and fixed on for execution at a certain day. At midnight or some hours later if found necessary, the men were to rise and overpower the guard, and having secured them, and possessed themselves of their arms, to separate into three distinct parties. The first of these, headed by one of the deputies, were to advance on the prison, and having effected our liberation, to hasten to the boats on the river, which the second division was to have secured; while the third, patrolling the streets in silence, were to prevent the inhabitants from assembling and impeding the operations of the first. This scheme, hastily adopted from the circumstances in which we found ourselves placed, was at best a wild one, since, had it succeeded in all its primary stages, we must have been eventually destroyed in descending the narrow river of the Scioto, by the fire from the numerous riflemen the enemy would have collected, on the first intimation of our departure. We were then, however, sanguine of success, and none paused to consider the difficulties that awaited us after our liberation, in the heart of an enemy's country, where ammunition and provisions were alike beyond our reach. We spoke of our descent of the Mississippi from the Scioto, and the Ohio, and our final reception on board the English fleet we knew to be cruising off New Orleans, as a matter of course, and discussed our meditated movements with all the confidence of the soldier, but certainly with little of the prudence or foresight of the general. Such was the plan decided on for our escape; but, while awaiting the completion of the necessary preparations, a circumstance, ludicrous in itself, yet alarming in our actual position, threatened to blight every hope by which we had lately been sustained. One morning about daybreak, the noise of workmen was distinctly heard beneath the windows of the room in which, covered with a solitary blanket, and huddled together without order or ceremony, we contrived to enjoy a few moments of repose. One of the party immediately jumped up, and running to the window, beheld a number of men engaged in the erection of a scaffold, The exclamation wrung from him by the sight, drew us all to the spot, and then, indeed, we might be said to have experienced the sensations of men who behold for the first time, and without a hope of reprieve, the gloomy preparations for an ignominious end. The predominant sentiment with us was, however, less regret for the existence we considered ourselves about to forfeit, than rage at the idea of having surrendered ourselves prisoners of war to an enemy capable of violating every principle of justice, for the sake of shielding a few perjured and despicable criminals from the laws of their offended country. In this state of cruel suspense, we continued until nine o'clock, the hour at which the bolts of our prison were withdrawn for the day, when the explanation given by the gaoler dissipated our alarm. The scaffolding was being erected for the purpose of sinking a pump for the use of the prison; and the indistinct view we had obtained of the construction through our bars had given rise to the error.

At length the much-wished-for day fixed on for the execution of our enterprise arrived, and we arose, as we fully hoped, from our couch of misery, for the last time. To persons in our situation, it may easily be imagined, the hours appeared to move on leaden wings, yet we doubted not an instant of a favorable result. Fate had, however, ordained otherwise. At four in the afternoon, while yet partaking of our wretched meal, the trampling of horses' feet, and a confused sound of drums and voices, drew us suddenly to the window, and in a few minutes we beheld Governor Shelby literally armed to the teeth, a rifle on his shoulder and accompanied by a numerous staff, riding up at full speed. We were for some time lost in astonishment and unable to account for this singular appearance; but a clue to the mystery was soon afforded by the entrance of an American officer, who, leaving his guard in the corridor, advanced into the outer room, accompanied by a formidable Cyclops, bearing certain insignia of his trade, with which we could very willingly have dispensed.

For the better insurance of success in our enterprise, it had been found necessary to admit two individuals in the town into our confidence —certain essential and preliminary arrangements remaining to be effected. These gentlemen were of the federal party, and entered into our views with a willingness which gave very fair promise of a favorable issue, We had been rather intimately known to them prior to our confinement, and with their sentiments, both political and private, we were well acquainted. The measures necessary to forward our undertaking were faithfully executed by them, and on the morning of the night which was to give us to liberty, as we fondly imagined, nothing of a preparatory nature remained to be done. Seized, however, by a sudden panic, and anticipating the consequences of a discovery of co-operation with the enemies of their country, they resolved to elude the danger they feared, by a voluntary and unreserved disclosure of our intentions to the Governor of the State, who resided in Chillicothe. This was accordingly done, and the active and precautionary measures consequent on this alarming intelligence, had given rise to the bustle and tumult which assailed our ears from without, and carried disappointment and despair to our hearts.

This latter information was conveyed to us by our new visitor, Lieutenant Harrison, of the 19th Infantry, a gentleman whose name I feel peculiar pleasure in recording, who now proceeded to communicate the disagreeable duty with which he was charged, and which the equipment of his forbidding attendant, armed with a hammer, anvil, and about twenty pairs of hand-cuffs, sufficiently explained. With a tearful eye and in a faltering tone, did this gentleman entreat us to lose sight of the man in the subordinate, and to believe how much it pained him to be the instrument selected for the purpose. Such an indignity, he said, he deplored being compelled to offer to British officers; but he trusted that with men to whom the rigour of military duty was familiar, the public act would be forgotten in the expression of private feeling. The delicacy of such conduct was felt by all, and we hastened to assure him of our grateful sentiments in return. He then desired the man to proceed to the execution of his office; and in less than an hour the hands of the whole party, myself alone excepted, were fettered with irons, which the rough and malignant-looking son of Vulcan seemed to feel no little satisfaction in applying. On inquiry, I learned that I had been excepted at the express desire of Colonel Campbell, commanding the troops at Chillicothe, from whom the order had emanated. For this favor I felt that I was indebted to my kind friend Mr. Brush, but as I had little inclination to be exempted from a participation in the fate of my companions, I expressed myself to that effect to Lieutenant Harrison, requesting at the same time that he would impart to the Commandant, who was the colonel of his own regiment, the utter disinclination I entertained to owe him any thing in the shape of obligation, while my brother officers were manacled as felons.

On the departure of the officer, we had full leisure to reflect on the hopelessness of our situation, and we inveighed not a little against the defection of our American friends, though, in fact, our own folly alone was to be taxed in having made the subjects of a country so interested in our detention accessory to the design. These reflections, however finally yielded to a feeling of mirth excited by the ludicrous appearance we exhibited, stalking about the room like spectres, and deprived of the usage of our arms, and we began to enjoy the panic partly visible to our eyes, and principally ascertained from our gaoler, from whose account it appeared large bodies of the inhabitants were already assembling to the sounds of the alarm drums and bugles. The guards and sentinels of our prison had been doubled at the first rumour, and the militia of the adjacent country were flocking in to strengthen the troops entrusted with the security of the men. It was not until a late hour in the night, that these warlike preparations appeared to be completed, the rolling of the drums frequently breaking on our ears, as we lay extended on our blankets, to which, after a close examination of our apartments by the gaoler, followed by an unusually careful application of bolts and keys, we had long since consigned our aching limbs.

In the state of utter helplessness to which my companions were reduced, we found the advantage of the exception made in my favour, since I was thus enabled to perform many little offices which the brutality and remissness of the gaoler left us no hope would be attended to by him. Three days had now elapsed since the visit of Lieutenant Harrison, when the situation of the sufferers had become irksome to a degree. Not once, during that period, had they been permitted to throw off their clothes, or perform their customary ablutions; and when they descended to the court, which was rarely and but for a few minutes, a sentinel followed with his bayonet extended, and within a foot of the prisoner. Their hands and wrists had also become extremely swollen by the compression of the irons, and the extremities of the fingers of several were discolored with the quantity of blood propelled to those parts. Under these circumstances I wrote a polite note to Colonel Campbell, detailing the several inconveniences sustained by my brother officers, and requesting that he would cause the fetters to be removed under the inspection of an officer, and merely for the time requisite to clean their persons and change their linen. To this communication I received a negative reply, couched in the most positive and unfeeling terms. I immediately wrote a second, expressive of our united sentiments in respect to his conduct, which I had no doubt would have brought down the wrath of the generous commandant on my head; but no notice whatever was taken of the letter. Finding it vain to expect any relief from this quarter, we adopted an expedient which answered all the intention proposed. With the aid of an old knife, we contrived to divide the nails by which the irons were riveted around the wrists, and substitute others of lead, a small quantity of which article one of the midshipmen happened to have in his haversack, The relief afforded by the removal of the fetters, which was only effected by stealth, and at those moments when we considered ourselves free from interruption, was grateful to all, though the fingers were so much cramped by the extended position in which they had been kept, as to render it difficult and painful to move them. The leaden pins had been blackened to imitate iron, and as the sleeves were carefully drawn over the wrists, the deception could only be discovered on a minute examination. Thus were the officers enabled not only to enjoy some little cessation from suffering, but to attend to the comfort and cleanliness of their persons, an advantage for which they certainly were not much indebted to the humanity of the public authorities of Chillicothe.

No. V

Nearly ten days had succeeded to the detection of our plan of escape, when, one evening at a late hour, we received intimation to prepare for our removal to the penitentiary of Frankfort in Kentucky, and accordingly the next day, about two o'clock in the afternoon, we were conducted to the front of the prison, where a detachment of regular infantry was drawn up with their ranks facing inwards, and at extended order. Between these ranks we were placed two abreast, and the detachment being ordered to face to the right and left, we moved on, thus escorted or rather enfiladed, from the gloomy walls of our prison. As if to humiliate us to the last degree, and add insult to misfortune, we were paraded through the principal streets of the town, though such a route was at once circuitous and unnecessary. The taunts and hisses of the populace who had assembled at an early hour to witness our departure, and were now with difficulty kept back by the guard, followed us throughout; but the clamorous ebullition of their hate gave us far less concern than the sombre countenances of the more respectable inhabitants, collected to view the passing scene. Those with whom we had lately associated, and who had exercised the courtesies of hospitality in our favour, now gazed upon us with various expression—some with a cold and triumphant disdain, originating in a false rumour, which had been industriously propagated, of a design to fire the town-others with evident interest and concern, arising from a conviction of the injustice of such a charge. Friends and foes were, however, alike to us at that moment, and the proud indifference of our looks lighted on all with the same cold expression; for we felt that the ignominious treatment to which we were then being subjected, reflected, not on us, who had attempted the fulfilment of a duty we owed both to our country and to ourselves, but on those who thus abused their power over us as defenceless captives. Still were we not without a secret confusion of soul, arising from the contrast of our late and actual positions, as we caught the long line of female heads which filled the windows and watched our approach with mingled emotions of curiosity and interest. From more than one of these the occasional and partial movement of a handkerchief or hand waved an adieu, which seemed apprehensive of detection; but manacled as we were, the eye alone could reply to the salutation. At length, when it was presumed that the good inhabitants of Chillicothe had sated themselves with a view of the "English lions," we were conducted to a large boat on the river, already manned with soldiers, and awaiting our arrival.

It was with a feeling of real pleasure that we found Lieutenant Harrison to be the officer in command of the detachment to whose charge we were here given over; and as we took our places, the boat was pushed off from the shore, and quickly glided down the Scioto, amid the continued hootings of the rabble, collected at the point of embarkation on its banks. Impressed with various reflections arising from the preceding scene, few of the party were disposed for conversation, and an almost uninterrupted silence had prevailed some hours, when, towards the close of the day, the boat struck against what is called in America a " sawyer," which is nothing more or less than the trunk of a tree carried off from the land during the floods, and frequently stationary in the beds of rivers, from whence, when acted on by the tides and currents, it rises suddenly to the surface in a perpendicular direction, preserving a state of reaction, and threatening destruction even to the largest boats used in the navigation of the Ohio and Mississippi. The concussion we experienced gave rise to serious apprehensions for our safety; and in an instant the leaden pins of the handcuffs were removed, but yet with sufficient precaution to escape the attention of the guard. Lieutenant Harrison, however, caused the boat to be directed towards the shore, and having expressed his intention to pass the night in an old deserted building which stood at the distance of some few hundred paces, we were accordingly disembarked. When arrived at the spot indicated for our temporary sojourn, the American officer, evidently impressed with a full sense of our recent danger, declared it to be his determination to remove the fetters from our hands, provided we would pledge our words to him, as British officers, that no attempt at escape should be made. This step, he observed, had not in any way the sanction of his superiors, but he was willing to take the responsibility upon himself, satisfied that our parole once engaged, no ultimate risk could be incurred. This circumstance, however grateful in fact, placed the manacled officers in a rather awkward dilemma, since it was evident that in removing the irons, which had been replaced the instant the danger was passed, the deception must be discovered. We had, however, formed too just an estimate of the character of Lieutenant Harrison to hesitate long in the avowal of a subterfuge to which we had been driven by suffering and necessity. Our promise was then given, and we once more enjoyed the unrestrained use of their limbs. At an early hour on the following morning we again embarked, and a few hours brought us to the point of confluence with the majestic waters of the Ohio. The strong current of this expansive river carried us rapidly forward, and we soon found ourselves at Cincinnati, the capital of the State. The first use we made of the momentary liberty obtained here, was to seek weapons of destruction against each other; for unhappily even during our painful confinement at Chillicothe, dissension had crept into our circle, and contributed to the unpleasantness of our situation. The parties in this case were Lieutenants Purvis, Stokoe and Rolette, all of the navy. Some warm discussions relative to the late engagement had given rise to a misunderstanding, which had terminated in the resolution to meet on the first favourable occasion. They were, however, of course much at a loss for pistols, it being quite out of the question to expect that the officer to whom the custody of our persons was entrusted, would so far commit his responsibility as to afford the means, or even admit of a duel taking place. In this dilemma recourse was had to an elderly officer, a major in the American regular service, who resided in the hotel where we stopped for the night. This gentleman unhesitatingly supplied all that was necessary for the occasion, and the first meeting took place at daybreak on the following morning. Purvis, who was the challenged party in both instances, received Rolette's fire with singular coolness, and then discharged his pistol in the air. His warm-hearted brother sailor immediately dashed his weapon to the earth, and heedless of cold formalities usual on such occasions, advanced to embrace him whom he still considered his companion and friend. Thus happily was the affair terminated. The second meeting took place some hours afterwards, and on the same spot; Mr. Garden, of the Newfoundland regiment, acting as the second of Purvis, I was the friend of Stokoe. In the same manner did the noble Purvis receive his adversary's fire; and nearly in the same manner, but with less effusion of feeling, were the brave sailors (one of whom, Stokoe, was scarcely recovered from a recent wound in the head) reconciled to each other. On our return towards the hotel, we found that a hue and cry had been raised in consequence of our absence; and even our friend Harrison, knowing not how to account for our sudden disappearance, had entertained no slight anxiety. Amidst the bustle and noise attendant on this circumstance, the gallant American major continued to preserve an honourable silence, and only avowed his participation when, on beholding us approach the inn with our ill-secreted weapons, he found there was no longer a necessity for concealment. At noon we again embarked, and the evening of that day was, in consequence of the reconciliation of all parties, the happiest we had passed for many weeks. Descending the full waters of the Ohio, we enjoyed the wild surrounding scenery, with additional and unbroken interest, while our guard amused themselves with firing at the numerous flocks of wild turkies which sprang up at every instant from either bank, and, winging their full and fearless flight over our heads, presented in their vast bulk an unerring mark to the murderous lead. After passing the boundary line which separates the States of Ohio and Kentucky, the direction of our course was changed, and we ascended a small river intersecting the latter state, and leading in the line of the capital. Our progress here was slow and difficult. A thick and apparently impervious wood skirted its banks, and, occasionally interweaving its protruding tops, threw a chilling gloom over the scene, while the close underwood, reaching to the very margin of the waters, seemed to preclude all possibility of a landing. At length a more open space was perceptible, and at this point our journey by water, owing to the increasing difficulty of movement, was discontinued. Horses were procured in the adjacent country; and, escorted by Lieutenant Harrison, who left his detachment in the boat, we continued our route towards Frankfort, then at no great distance. After traveling through a wild and thinly inhabited country, and along paths which no other than American horses could have trod with safety, a range of lofty and gloomy hills, by which that capital is nearly surrounded, announced the proximity of what we were to consider as our future home. The morning was cold and rainy, and as we wound round the base of a hill which intercepted our view, the towering walls of the penitentiary, situated in the extremity of the town by which we approached, fell suddenly on our gaze. A few minutes brought us on a line with its principal entrance; and as we glanced upwards at the low and narrow windows, we beheld our companions thrusting their handkerchiefs through the bars and saluting us as they could. They were the party that had preceded us from Chillicothe, and consisted chiefly of the officers taken at Moraviantown. It was a melancholy moment for recognition, and our feelings had imbibed much of the sombre character of the season, as we moved on to the spot appointed for our deliver into the hands of the marshal. This duty performed, Lieutenant Harrison bade us adieu, with a friendly warmth which every individual in our party fully appreciated and returned. Should these pages ever meet the eye of that officer, he may perceive that his gentlemanly and humane conduct throughout has not been lost on the captives entrusted under such painful circumstances to his care. May he be induced to consider the testimony of one as the unqualified sentiment of all!

On entering the prison of the penitentiary, we found our friends distributed into two small rooms little larger than common cells, and crowded together in a distressing manner; but many had reconciled themselves to their situations, and enjoyed a temporary distraction in studying the trades carried on by the convicts in the court, who cheerfully initiated them into the rudiments of their respective arts. Our stay here, however, was too limited to admit of perfection in our occupations.

At this period a strong sensation was produced in America by the intelligence of Napoleon's unexpected reverses in Russia. A termination of the war between Great Britain and France might now be anticipated as an event of no very remote occurrence, and the ability thus afforded to the former power of sending a more formidable army to oppose that of the United States would place the struggle between the two countries on a very different footing. Under this view of the case, and as one of the measures consequent on the altered aspect of the war, the affair of the hostages was gradually suffered to die away. The first step, however, was only an amelioration of our condition, which was effected by our removal from the penitentiary to the town. The principal hotel in Frankfort, to which was attached an extensive garden, surrounded by a low wall, was the place selected for our residence, with the express prohibition, however, of outstepping its limits. Here our sufferings were in a great measure at an end, and on the score of personal comfort we had no reason to complain. Three shillings a day was the allowance granted by the American government to each officer, and the sick were entitled to twice that amount. With the first sum we were boarded in the hotel. One room was occupied by two prisoners, and our table was abundantly supplied with excellent food. Tea, coffee, eggs, cold meat, and the various "sweet sauces" to which the Americans are so partial, composed our breakfast; while at dinner we generally found ourselves seated before meats of every description, interspersed with game and "long sauce," (by this is to be understood potatoes and other vegetables,) and succeeded by a plentiful dessert, two large decanters of whisky invariably occupying their stations at either extremity of the table. Of this latter article, however, our consumption was small, it being extremely fiery, and possessing few of the properties of that of the lands of the thistle and shamrock. Tea, coffee, and hot cakes, such as at sea I have often with an envious eye beheld descending for the breakfast of the ship's officers, while compelled myself to eat the dry and mouldy fragments from the bread-room, composed our evening repast. A number of black slaves were also at our orders, and the washing of our linen was included in the moderate charge. Such was the revolution effected in our position, and but for the restraint imposed on our liberty, our chains would have been light. Our promenade was the garden, and as some of the officers still retained their uniforms, we were the objects of general attraction to the long-bodied and long-limbed backwoodsmen of Kentucky, assembled daily to behold the "British," who, much to the surprise of many, were discovered to be of the same colour with themselves, and not like the "Ingians," as they had been taught to believe. Their rude and unceremonious stare generally drew from us boisterous expressions of mirth and ridicule,—the only arms we found successful in driving them from us; and on these occasions they would exclaim to each other in evident surprise, and in their usual nasal drawling tone, "Tarnation seize me if these Britainners don't treat us more as if we were their prisoners than they ours;" "Roar me up a sapling if they arnt mighty saucy;" "By Ch—t I've the swiftest horse, the truest rifle and the prettiest sister in the whole state of Kentucky, but I'd give 'em all to have one long shot;" and other equally expressive phrases peculiar to themselves. To be gazed at like wild beasts, and to be constantly interrupted in our seclusion, was not altogether desirable, but we were compelled to submit to their impertinent curiosity, and were sometimes gratified in return by a "biting and gouging" match. This mode of fighting is very common in this Western State, where many a disgusting victim of its practice may be encountered. When two combatants engage in this strife, the principal manoeuvre is to grasp the hair pending over the temples, and worn of an unusual length by the lower orders of people. The forefinger of each hand is then twisted into it in such a manner as to form a *point d'appui*, and the thumb being dexterously inserted into the eye, every effort is made to remove it from the socket. The next object of attack is the nose, and ill-fated is the wretch who in a moment of hostility suffers this member to fall between the teeth of his adversary. To crown the honour of the disgusting exhibition, blows from the feet are directed towards a particular part of the individual, where injury is certain and agonizing death. It is by no means uncommon to see men in these States deprived of portions of their noses; and on our route at a period subsequent to that which I now treat, we fell in with a man who had lost not only his nose, but presented a terrific example of this horrible species of combat, in the wild distortion of eyes half wrested from their sockets.

At length, in consequence of an order from the seat of Government, we were once more placed on parole, and permission was accorded to such of the prisoners as chose to pay their own expenses, and provide their own horses, to repair to the Canadian frontier. This offer was eagerly embraced by the field officers and such others as the state of their finances would permit. The remainder were compelled to await the definitive arrangements then in agitation for an exchange of prisoners, hoping that the shackles of captivity, which had at the outset promised to be of long continuance, would speedily be removed; and we availed ourselves of the liberty once more accorded. Several gentlemen of the highest respectability in the place were forward in offering attention; and among the first of these was Major Madison. This officer had been himself a prisoner in Lower Canada, from whence he was only recently returned, and, impressed with a grateful sense of the treatment he had received, hastened to evince it by various acts of hospitality and courtesy towards ourselves. We became welcome visitors in his family, and frequently accompanied him in excursions to several delightful country seats at some distance from the town. Permission was frequently obtained for us to visit places at the distance of twenty miles without any escort whatever; and as our purses had been replenished by the kindness of Mr. Sproule, a Frankfort banker, without any other guarantee for future payment than our simple bills, these excursions were not few. A good understanding was, however, only maintained with a very small portion of the inhabitants. By the rest we were regarded with an eye of jealousy and detestation, and whenever opportunities did present themselves, these feelings were undisguisedly manifested, though it must be confessed we took little pains to conciliate them, but, on the contrary treated them with a hauteur bordering on contempt. We had made it an invariable rule to celebrate the festivals of our tutelar saints, and the anniversary of the King's birthday we resolved to keep as became liege and royal subjects. Our dining-room, the windows of which were thrown open on account of the excessive heat, overlooked one of the principal streets, and as we had substituted our uniforms for the grey cotton frocks, which, like the Kentucky riflemen, we generally wore, our preparations were viewed with an increased feeling of disquietude and dislike. In no way awed by the forbidding air of the crowd collected in front of our hotel, and little inclined to forego the customary tribute of respect to our sovereign, our toasts were adapted to the occasion, although by no means suited to the fastidious taste of our listeners. This, however, was endured until towards Britannia," fell in startling numbers on their ears. Unable to contain their wrath and impatience, they rushed forward to the entrance hall, but were prevented ascending the stairs by our host Mr Weisiger, who knew his own interest too well to suffer men who paid him thirty dollars a dozen for Claret and twenty-four for Madeira, and consumed no small quantity of either, to be thus unceremoniously disturbed. An innkeeper is a man of no mean importance in the United States, and the persuasions of Mr. Weisiger had their effect. They retired, but with a threat of future vengeance. That threat was speedily executed, and in a manner worthy of themselves.

As a slight return for the attentions of Major Madison, Lieutenant Irvine of the Navy, the person so honorably alluded to in the first part of this narrative, had, with an ingenuity for which he was remarkable, constructed a vessel in miniature for the daughter of that gentleman. To many of the inhabitants of Kentucky the model even of a frigate complete in all her parts, was a novel sight, and the present was thankfully received. Anxious to tender a similar offering, though in a different quarter, a young midshipman named Campbell, occupying one of the upper rooms, had undertaken a similar task, and devoting himself with all the anxiety and ardor of his years to the completion of his vessel, soon had the satisfaction of seeing it in a state of great forwardness. Most unfortunately for him, however, he had forgotten that an English flag, even on a bark of those Lilliputian dimensions, is ever an offensive image to an American eye; and decked in this fatal ornament, it now lay exposed in one of the windows of his apartment, and was distinctly visible from the street. On the morning of its exhibition, a crowd of persons, delighted at having what they conceived a pretext for insult, rushed in a body up the stairs, uttering imprecations and threats. Having reached the spot where the object of their fury was lying, they seized the luckless ship, and dashed it on the pavement of the street, where it was shattered in a thousand fragments, the leader of the party exclaiming, "You d—d British rascals, if you show your d—m—d colours here again, we'll throw you after them." This noble feat being accomplished, they retired, swearing at us all in true Kentucky style, and leaving poor Campbell to brood at leisure over his misfortune,

Shortly after this event, arrived the agreeable intelligence of a general exchange of prisoners; and a few evenings previous to our departure another act of hostility, though of a more personal and revengeful nature, was directed towards myself. Since our liberation on parole, I had been rather intimate in the family of a highly esteemed and much lamented officer, who had fallen in the affair of Frenchtown in the preceding year. Among the persons whom I occasionally met beneath this hospitable roof, was a Mr. James, a man of vulgar bearing and appearance, and evidently little used to the decorum necessary to be preserved in the society of females. I had ever cautiously avoided all sort of immediate connexion with this person, for whom I felt the most decided dislike, but could not on one occasion forbear commenting aloud on the ungentlemanly tenor of his conduct in persisting to smoke a cigar in the drawing-room, to the evident annoyance of the females of the family. He made no reply to my observation, but, darting a look full of malignant meaning, soon rose from his seat and retired. From this period, he seemed cautiously to avoid me, and we never afterwards met under the same roof. When the order for our departure reached Frankfort, many of the officers employed the intermediate time in farewell visits to their acquaintance. The last evening but one prior to our journey, I passed with the family in question, and only left them at a very advanced hour of the night. The house was situated in an unfrequented part of the town, and my path lay along a solitary declivity leading to the foot of our garden wall. I had not advanced more than a hundred yards, when through the gloom I perceived a man stationary near the road. The unusual appearance of this person at such an hour somewhat startled me, yet I resolved to see who it was. My suspense was not of long duration. The figure proved to be Mr. James, who now placed himself in such a manner as to bar my passage. I endeavoured to avoid him, and demanded the motive of his conduct. This, he said, I should presently know, and swearing a horrid oath, observed, "You have escaped me once, but I'll take good care you don't again." His right hand grasped a stiletto or dirk, which he held behind his back, and with the other he made a sudden movement to seize me by the collar. I felt all the danger of my situation, and found that, unarmed as I was, and opposed to a man whose physical strength exceeded my own, my only chance of safety was in flight. The thought was no sooner conceived than executed, and, eluding his touch, I ran with all the speed of one who perceives that life hangs on the fleetness of his steps. This unexpected movement rather disconcerted my enemy, but he speedily recovered from his surprise; and on his uttering a shrill whistle, several other persons sprang up from an ambuscade on either side of the road, and joined in the pursuit. Not a cry was uttered—not a sound broke on the stillness of the night, save that of rapid and numerous footsteps; for I felt that ay exclamation for assistance would be too late, and that one desperate attempt alone could save me. If fear sometimes deprives me of the power of action, it also sometimes urges them to undertake seeming impossibilities. The garden-wall which I now rapidly approached, was upwards of five feet in height, and the ground leading to it from the outside sloped rather abruptly off its base. At any other moment I should not have thought of attempting it, but a successful leap was now my only hope of escape. Placing my left hand on the wall, I made a desperate bound, and cleared it with ease which surprise me even at that moment; and, as I was in the act of passing, I felt my coat glide from the uncertain grasp of one of my pursuers. Nor was this all the effect produced by a sense of danger. Impressed with an idea that my enemies were still in pursuit, I stopped not an instant in my flight, but advanced to the opposite extremity of the garden. The gate which opened into the court was firmly closed, but such was the violence with which I thrust my person against it, that it fell as if entirely unsupported; nor did I discontinue my speed until I had finally gained my apartment.

On the following day I despatched a note to Mrs. H— with an account of the assassination meditated by Mr. James; and received a reply towards the close of the evening, filled with expressions of concern at the occurrence, and stating that their doors were in consequence closed against him for ever; and the letter contained other intelligence of a more important nature. Foiled in his attempt of the preceding evening, and enraged at the affront thus offered him by the family, the ruffian had that morning boldly avowed having followed me to Lexington in the same State, where I had some time previously accompanied a brother-officer,[4] for the purpose of witnessing the ascent of a balloon, with a brace of pistols in his pocket, and with the fixed determination to shoot me in the crowd, an object which had only been left unaccomplished from the circumstances of his having lost sight of my person. This assertion, the letter intimated, there was every reason to believe correct; and I was now enabled to account for his expression, "You have

[4] Lieut. (now Captain) Watson, and residing in London.

escaped me once, but I'll take good care you don't again." I now began to think my life seriously endangered, and but for the circumstance of our departure having been fixed on for the following day, should have been compelled to call on the authorities of the place for protection. We were not permitted to have arms of any kind in our possession, and not one of our apartments was provided with a key or fastening of any description. Nothing therefore could be more easy than for an assassin to find his way to his victim in this unguarded building; and it was under the firm impression of a visit of this nature that I retired for the last time to my place of rest. Nor was it until the day had some time dawned, that I ventured to consign my wearied senses to the repose they so much required. Such was my adventure with this individual; and although it may appear extraordinary, it is no less true, that I had no reason to believe any other motive for his vindictive conduct existed, than that I have already mentioned.

The morning of our departure from Frankfort was one of joy and exultation to us all; and at any early hour most of the officers were already up and preparing for the journey. Those alone who have experienced the miseries and restraints attendant on a state of captivity, especially under such circumstances as those by which that of the officers of the right division was marked, can enter into the feelings by which we were actuated. By many the news, although long expected, of our exchange being actually effected, had been received as a pleasing dream or illusion, from which the mind dreaded to be awakened; and until the moment of actual departure, that restlessness of impatience which is the offspring of uncertainty seemed to dominate in every breast. A thousand things unlikely to occur, but still within the pale of possibility, presented themselves to imaginations more disposed to the expectation of gloomy than of agreeable events. The order for our departure might be repealed—the negotiation for the exchange broken off altogether—and to crown all, the cruel subject of the hostages renewed. Pleasurable anticipations belong only to those who have basked in the unbroken sunshine of Fortune—those who have been tutored in the school of Adversity are less sanguine in their hopes, and temper the glow of generous confidence with the steady calm of waning experience.

Our horses were at length brought to the entrance of the hotel, before which nearly half the town of Frankfort had collected to witness our departure. Habited in our light Kentucky frocks, fastened by silver buckles attached to broad red morocco belts, we soon vaulted into the saddle; and escorted by Lieutenant Mitchell of the rifle service, and Mr. Crocket, the marshal of the state, a consequential gentleman, who had often vainly sought to subdue our refractory spirits into something like submission to his authority, we commenced our journey. The hand of kindness and the voice of gentlemanly consideration were extended to us by a few, among whom stood principally conspicuous Major Madison and the banker Mr. Sproule; but on the countenances of the many might be traced very different feelings. Even while detesting our presence, they seemed to regret the approaching removal of their victims, and the insolence of their looks and observations bore sufficient testimony of their hostility. A more serious apprehension, however, than that of looks and comments weighed with me at the moment; for I fully expected to be in some measure compelled to run the gauntlet in the wood through which we were to pass. The character of the villain who had already meditated two several attacks on my life was such as to excite a belief that I should be greeted with a parting "long shot" from a rifle, an impression which several of my brother officers shared with me; and for the first league of our journey we examined every tree as we passed with a scrutinizing glance, frequently casting a look behind to see if the assassin was not in cautious pursuit. Nothing however occurred.

Pursuing a route different from that by which we had reached Frankfort, we soon arrived at Newport, a small town situated at the confluence of the Kanaway and Ohio rivers, and immediately opposite to Cincinnati, in the neighborhood of which latter place the prisoners from Chillicothe were awaiting the arrival of their officers. Large boats were procured for the passage of our horses, and having crossed the river the same evening, we were conducted to our old quarters, the principal hotel in Cincinnati. While passing through the streets, we observed several groups of people collected, and evidently discussing some subject if interest. A gloomy expression of disappointment seemed to hang on every brow, and, as the evening advanced, the groups became more numerous. With the knowledge we had of the rage for politics which distinguishes every class, age, and sex, in the United States, we immediately conjectured that the "British" had gained some serious advantage over them, and our idea proved to be correct; for on inquiry at the hotel we found that this violent sensation had been produced by intelligence just received of the capture of the Essex frigate near Valparaiso. This was felt as a severe blow by the Americans, whose successes at sea at the outset had led them to imagine their power invincible on that element; and the only consolation they now derived, arose from an assertion, eagerly spread as eagerly accredited by the vulgar, that their beloved frigate had only yielded to the united efforts of two English vessels of war, each of which was of sufficient force to cope singly with her enemy. This unpleasant news did not, however, retard certain preparations we found making at the hotel for a ball the same evening; and soon after our arrival, several of our regimental band entered to say that they had been desired by the American officers to be in attendance for the evening,—a command which they had refused to obey, unless the sanction of their own officers was obtained. We had, throughout the whole period of our activity, carried what the Americans were pleased to call a very high hand, and been at some pains to show them that even as prisoners we expected to be treated as gentlemen; and that there were certain points of etiquette which we were not willing to wave. This was decidedly one; and as they had not evinced delicacy enough to go through the form of asking a permission which would have been unhesitatingly accorded, we expressed our disapprobation of the proceeding, and the band positively refused to attend. This decision gave much umbrage to the party. Yet, as it was by no means our intention to deprive the ladies of their amusement, but simply to remind the American officers that, although prisoners, the men were not to be ordered about as slaves or to be held amenable to their will in cases unconnected with our actual position, we subsequently repealed the prohibition, authorizing them at the same time to state the motives of our conduct if questioned by the former. The weak orchestra of Cincinnati had therefore the addition of our imperfect band, and harmony appeared to be the order of the evening. The apartment we occupied was in a distinct angle of the building, but opening into a corridor communicating with the ballroom; and two or three American gentlemen, whom we had previously known, having been invited to join our circle, the hours flew rapidly by in conviviality and cheerful converse. The bottle circulated freely, but without leading to excess, and songs were finally introduced. Two or three had already been sung, when an American officer, smarting in all probability beneath the loss of the Essex and the recollection of our recent lesson of politeness, appeared at the door to say that we were disturbing the dancers, and desired our silence. With this very modest request we declined to comply, observing that we were, like themselves, in a public inn, forming a distinct society, and in no way disposed to forego the pleasure of our meeting at so peremptory an intimation. The intruder then thought proper to use some threatening expressions, which were answered by Lieutenant Clements, of the 41st, to whom they were addressed. The language of hostility he was told, in an ironical tone, well became him, who, powerful only in our weakness, and abusing the position in which we were placed, thus ventured to give utterance to his sentiments; and after some farther observations he withdrew without advancing his object. We were soon afterwards, however, visited by our redoubtable "guardian," Mr. Crocket, who, burning for an opportunity to display a little of his now expiring authority, entered the apartment with due and becoming solemnity of voice and manner, repeating the order of the person who had preceded him. Finding us, however, as usual, refractory, and Clements in particular, he pompously threatened to detain that officer altogether, and suffer the rest of the party to proceed without him. The impotency of this threat called up an incredulous and provoking smile on the countenance of Clements, accompanied by a "Just as you please, Mr. Crocket—we know you to be a man of authority," which irritated the Marshall beyond bearing. Pale with rage, and in a voice broken by agitation, he returned, "Another word, sir, and I shall drag you to prison." "Just as you please, Mr. Crocket—we know you to be a man of authority;" and the same sarcastic smile accompanied the reply.—"Silence, sir, or you go to prison this very instant."—"Just as you please, Mr Crocket—we know you to be a man of authority;" and he sipped his wine, and held his glass up to the light with an air of provoking composure and indifference. "Follow me, Mr. Clements," vociferated the indignant Marshal. Clements drank off his wine, rose slowly from his seat, threw on his hat with an air of nonchalance, wished us a "good night," and left the apartment with another cutting "We know you to be a man of authority, Mr. Crocket." There was nothing in the mere words, but the tone of irony in which they were drawled forth, the manner which accompanies them, and the personal contempt they conveyed, stung the angry Kentuckian to the soul. We saw no more of our companion until the following morning, when, visiting the gaol of Cincinnati at an early hour, we found him lying on the floor, dressed as he had left us, and wrapped in a blanket which had been given him by the gaoler. He was then enjoying a profound sleep in the apartment, which he shared with two other prisoners; the one was a robber, the other a reputed murderer!

The morning of Clements' liberation was the last of Mr. Crocket's "guardianship;" for we were now handed over to an old friend, Mr. Steele, the Marshal of Ohio, a man as gentle, considerate, and unassuming, as the other was harsh, exacting, and overbearing. From this gentleman we received an account of the death of our old persecutor Colonel Campbell. This officer had been desperately wounded on the Niagara frontier, whither he had been ordered with his regiment soon after our departure from Chillicothe. The cap of his knee had been carried away by a cannon shot, and he died in extreme agony. If we had humanity enough not to rejoice at this intelligence, we certainly did not indulge in any very immoderate grief; for the unfeeling conduct of that individual was still fresh in the recollection of many, and above all the insult of exposing us to public curiosity in the principal streets of a town in which he held the first military command—an insult we had every reason to believe originated with himself.

On joining the men, we found, that independently of those whom the Americans had successfully employed every art to seduce from our service, two individuals were missing, in whose fate we had become previously interested. At the moment of departure from the harbour of Amherstburg, Captain Barclay had received two young Indian warriors, anxious to witness a naval combat, on board of the Detroit; and on engaging the American fleet, they were stationed in the tops with their rifles. This position, however, they found less secure than the trees of their native forests, and were soon assailed by showers of grape and canister which filled them with dismay. They instantly relinquished their rifles, and hastened to decamp. Too much frightened to adopt the safer and more usual mode of descent by the ladder of the rigging, they each grasped a loose rope pending from the yards, and in this manner glided with fearful rapidity to the deck, lacerating their hands in a cruel manner, and no doubt secretly regretting their spirit of adventure. Nor did they stop until they reached the bottom of the hold, where they were subsequently found by the Americans, lying within a large coil of rope, and in company with a pet bear, belonging to one of the crew, who had conveyed him there as a place of perfect security from the enemy's shot. In our occasional visits to the encampment at Chillicothe, we always saw and conversed with them, and at the last which preceded our close imprisonment, we found them busily engaged in making bows and arrows—a work in which they were not interrupted by their guard, who probably saw nothing more in the occupation than amusement, or an agreeable employment of their time, but they told us in their own tongue, a little of which was understood by one or two of the party, that they were meditating their escape, and that the bows and arrows were to provide them with food in the woods. The intelligence now received was, that they had succeeded in effecting their design shortly after our departure, having managed to scale the picketing on a dark night, which they had selected for the purpose. What the final result of their enterprise was, we had no future opportunity of ascertaining; but with the knowledge we possessed of the extreme facility with which the Indians find their way through the deepest and most extensive forests, we did not entertain a doubt of their having rejoined their countrymen in safety.

Our route from Cincinnati lay through the same dull region we had traversed the preceding autumn; but with feelings far different from those we then experienced, did we now measure back our steps. The season too was changed, and instead of chill damps and penetrating rains, over the face of nature was spread the genial warmth of summer. It was the middle of July: and though the ardent rays of a burning sun threw their oppressive lustre on our heads, while traversing the more open parts of the country, we much more frequently found shelter in thick and extensive woods where a solitary, winding and imperfect wagon-road alone marked the progress of civilization. Each moment of our journey brought us nearer to the more fortunate companions of our toils, and the final termination of our anxieties; and with this heart-cheering perspective we reconciled ourselves to the privations we were again compelled to endure along this inhospitable road. A detachment of American infantry escorted the men, and with the officers we were on more friendly terms than at any other previous period, nor did our normal good understanding suffer the slightest interruption to the end. Among themselves, however, the spirit of discord had been let loose, and we witnessed an exhibition of physical strength soon after our journey commenced, against which as men our hearts recoiled, and for which as British officers we were wholly at a loss to account. A quarrel had arisen shortly after our departure from Cincinnati between Doctor Baldwin and Lieutenant Edmondson, both of the same regiment, and attached to the escorting party, which terminated in a challenge from the former. Edmondson, from some particular motive refused to accept it, and Baldwin, even on the route, caused placards of the affair to be printed and posted in one of the towns at which we stopped for the evening. Edmondson, who had clearly been stigmatized with the name of 'coward,' received the account of this proceeding with apparent calmness and indifference, and the Doctor evidently exulted in his victory. On the following morning while we were all seated at the breakfast-table, Edmondson whispered his adversary that he had something to communicate to him, and requested a private interview. Baldwin instantly arose and followed to a considerable distance from the inn. The heat of the weather was oppressive, and he had thrown off both coat and waistcoat on sitting down to breakfast, neither of which he resumed on retiring. After having gained a retired spot, Edmondson, who had hitherto preserved an unbroken silence, suddenly stopped and sternly desired his now alarmed enemy to take off his shirt. This the other refused; and Edmondson, who was a very powerful and active young man, caught him by the collar of this slight garment and exhibiting a strong cowhide, which he drew from within the sleeve of his coat, proceeded to use it in a cruel manner. In vain did Baldwin, whose person was weak and diminutive, make the most desperate efforts to escape the grasp of his antagonist, or with entreaties for mercy seek to disarm the vengeance of his oppressor. The strokes fell without intermission on his back and shoulders; and when several of our party, alarmed at their long absence and apprehending some serious termination of their conference, moved in the direction they had taken, they beheld the unfortunate Baldwin writhing beneath the lash and uttering prayers for delivery, intermingled with imprecations, which were utterly disregarded by Edmondson, whose heart was steeled against pity, and whose cool, collected countenance contrasted singularly with the agitation and despair visible on that of his victim. As the intruders approached, he ceased; but not until the unhappy Baldwin had been fearfully lacerated. Filled with rage and humiliation at this treatment, the sufferer was no sooner released, than he swore that Edmondson's life should pay forfeit of his temerity; and so well did the latter believe in an attempt at the fulfillment of this threat, that during the remainder of the journey he never retired to repose in his tent without placing his loaded pistols at his side, and using every other precaution to guard against surprise. How the affair subsequently terminated, we had no opportunity of knowing; but during the period that we continued with them, the rankling hatred of these officers was indulged in secret, and manifested in no other way than by looks that would have murdered if they could, whenever they came in contact with each other.

Towards the close of August we again arrived at Sandusky, and during nearly the whole of the succeeding month, were compelled to remain encamped on the small marshy plain extending from the base of the hill on which that fort is situated, to the edge of the river from which it derives its name. Owing to the unjustifiable neglect of those to whom that office was entrusted, not a boat was in readiness for our transportation across the lake, and we beheld this new and unlooked-for evil with dismay. The finishing stroke was put to our calamities by the introduction of intermittent fever into the camp, a malady which necessarily arose from constant exposure to heavy fogs and noxious exhalations from the stagnant waters around us. Few of the officers escaped this cruel and distressing scourge, and nearly one-half of the men were attacked by it. With the view of having the former more immediately at hand, the medical officers in the fort caused them to be conducted to a small building contiguous to one of the gates, which had been previously used as a stable, and admitted the air and rain on every side. A handful of hay, covered with a blanket, composed our couch; and here, in a state of inexpressible misery, did we languish beneath the effects of accumulating privation and disease. Nourishing or refreshing aliment we were utterly unable to obtain, and the absence of necessary medicaments was severely felt. Either from ignorance or indolence, but we were given to presume the former, the medical officers, while they prescribed bleeding, would not perform that office themselves, but entrusted it to a drummer of the garrison, who certainly, to his credit be it said, opened our veins with admirable dexterity. This operation being performed on the arm of each patient, half a pint of raw whisky was given us to drink. If this potation was administered with an idea of burning the disease out, the effect did not answer the intention, for our stomachs were long inflamed in consequence of this draught, and the fever raged with unceasing violence. Heartily sick of our present abode, we begged to be removed to the tents we had lately occupied. This request was accorded; but here we were visited by another severe inconvenience. The neighbourhood of Sandusky abounded in wolves, and our ears were nightly assailed with their dismal howlings. The noise generally commenced from one pack at no great distance from the fort, and was repeated by several others in succession, and from opposite directions, until the whole extent of surrounding woods appeared to be alive with them. There was something fearfully gloomy in this association of wild sounds, particularly when the night was far advanced, and the encampment hushed into silence and repose, yet but for the danger actually apprehended, we should have been disposed to find amusement in their discordant yellings; for these bold animals came frequently down from the adjacent hills, and by the pale light of the dying embers, we could distinctly see and hear them crunching the bones and fragments remaining from our meals. At our repeated solicitations, however, firearms were accorded us; and though we made no actual use of them, they inspired us with a feeling of greater confidence and security. Yet were we not even then entirely free from alarm, especially as our tents were detached at some distance from each other; and more than one sleepless night did we pass with our fingers on the triggers of our muskets, and momentarily expecting to be attacked by these ravenous prowlers, against whose fury we invariably took the precaution to secure the entrance to our tents in every possible manner.

Our situation was now become truly pitiable, and some of the officers were compelled to part with their scanty wardrobe, in order to procure the common necessaries of life, from the few miserable settlers who had taken up their abode in the neighborhood of the fort, which they partially supplied with milk and vegetables. The former article was that most in requisition with the invalids, and, in addition to the wild fruits which we ate with avidity, contributed not a little to the increase of our malady. At length when nearly worn down by vain expectation and undermining fever, a solitary boat was seen slowly emerging from one of the angles formed by the windings of the narrow and unhealthy river, and in this we were embarked for Cleveland, a small harbour on the American shore, opposite to Long Point, in Canada, where we were to be finally delivered up. During this coasting voyage, we were assailed by a tempest which upset our boat; but as we had fortunately kept close to the land, the accident occurred in water not beyond our depth, and we easily succeeded in righting and dragging the vessel to the shore. Every article of clothing was, however, completely wet through, and no habitation being near, we were compelled to throw ourselves for the night on the damp beach, covered with blankets still dripping with recent wet, and suffering the extremes of cold and heat, as the various stages of our disease were developed. It required more than ordinary constitutions to resist these attacks, and one officer (Lieutenant Jones, of the 41st) subsequently perished. Our provisions had been utterly destroyed by the water, and our only dependence was on the scanty pittance obtained from the impoverished inhabitants along the coast. A few potatoes and a small quantity of rancid butter were all that could be procured by the American officer escorting us, and these we devoured with all the keenness and rapacity of famished wolves; yet was our hunger never wholly appeased. At length the harbour of Cleveland appeared in sight, and we were now landed on the beach, where several of the officers imprudently ate large quantities of peaches which grew uninclosed and in abundance around. The accession of fever produced in consequence was great, and the night was passed in the ravings of a delirium little short of madness. On the following morning we were re-embarked in a small vessel lying in the harbour; and leaving Lieutenant Watson behind to await the arrival, and superintend the transportation of the men who were advancing by land, we again set sail. Long Point, the place of our destination, was soon gained; but with what altered feelings did we now behold that soil which, one short month before, would have been hailed with rapturous exultation! Disease had worn away our persons, and our minds were deeply tinged with that morbid melancholy which is a characteristic feature in the complaint. Existence itself had nearly lost its value with its charms, and, in our then tone of feeling, liberty or captivity were situations of indifference. It had rained without intermission during the passage, and on the vessel being brought to anchor, we were summoned from the small filthy cabin, into which we had been thrown, to the boats waiting for our reception. In a few minutes we were landed, exhibiting to those by whom we were received on the beach the most distressing images of poverty, disease, exhaustion, and discontent. We arrived in Canada on the 4th of October, 1814, making just one year from the date of our captivity.

A word in conclusion, of our complaint. The ague we had contracted was of the most tormenting and dangerous description. Several of the officers continued to be afflicted with it for five successive months; and during that period not one day of respite was experienced. The cold fit generally commenced about four o'clock in the afternoon, and was preceded by excessive hunger, which it did not afford time to appease. It continued with dreadful shiverings, accompanied by distortions of the features, until seven, at which hour fever and delirium resumed their empire, raging with intolerable violence, and causing the sufferer frequently to start in agony from his burning couch and rush into the open air. This usually lasted longer than the cold fit, and was succeeded by a languor and torpor of the senses amounting almost to imbecility. Arsenic was copiously administered to several, yet without effect; but large quantities of Peruvian bark infused in Port wine proved an efficient remedy. The evil stopped not here. The disease was accompanied by dysentery, and ended with many in an affection of the spleen. The succeeding winter being also extremely severe, greatly retarded our convalescence; and for months after our liberation we dragged on a joyless, cheerless existence, equally insensible to the attentions of our friends and to the amusements by which we were everywhere surrounded while in winter quarters, and in which our more fortunate companions, who had preceded us from Frankfort, indulged. At length Spring with her smiling and invigorating attributes arrived to dissipate the remnants of the disease, and restore us to that cheerfulness, of which we had long been deprived; and when, after the cessation of hostilities between England and America, a great proportion of the Canadian troops received the order for embarkation to join the English army in Flanders, we were once more enabled to prepare for fresh toils, and enter with renewed ardour on the duties of our profession.

THE END.

National Gazette and Literary Register, [Philadelphia, Pa.] August 7, 1827.

To the Editor of the *National Gazette*

Sir, In your paper of the 2nd and 11th instant, I read the 6th Number of a series of narrative articles, under the head of a "Canadian Campaign" by a British officer. Will you allow one, who feels some interest in the State whose citizens are principally treated in that article, to make a few observations on it through your columns.

That the incidents the British officer relates as occurring in Frankfort, Ky. may be properly understood, it is dispensable that a few words should be said explanatory of the peculiar feelings which the Kentuckians at that time held towards the British officers in the Canadian service.

Late in January 1812, a detachment of the northwestern army of the United States chiefly composed of Kentucky volunteers, under the command of Gen. Winchester, had an engagement at Frenchtown on the banks of the River Raisin, with the combined British and Indian forces, amounting to almost double their numbers, under the command of General Proctor. Winchester and one of his principal officers were surprised and captured by the enemy, in a building without the lines of the encampment, before the battle commenced. The command of our forces devolved upon Major Madison, who gave so bloody an encounter to the enemy, that he had despaired of success by arms, and determined to draw off his forces, if he failed in the stratagem of demanding a surrender, which he accompanied with the threat of yielding his prisoners—General Winchester and Col. Lewis—in event of refusal, to the savages, and with the statement that General W. ordered them to surrender—Major Madison, expecting a renewal of the engagement if he held out, and finding that his ammunition was very nearly expended, capitulated on honorable terms. Instantly the Indians rushed among our men, and commenced most unceremoniously, stripping them of watches, clothes, canteens, etc. Major M. remonstrated. He was answered by the enemy that he could not control the savages. “Then,” replied Madison, “I can. Men to your arms!” soon driving the Indians to a respectful distance; Proctor now came forward, gave the strongest and most solemn assurances of fair dealing, and of protection from the savages—if we would ground our arms; promised that a detachment of British soldiers should remain, charged with the comfort and safety of the wounded.

No sooner were our men unarmed, than the Indians were let loose among them, massacring more than half their numbers. The remainder the British carried with them to Malden, except those whose wounds disabled them from traveling on foot. These were crowded into an out-house, and, not withstanding Proctor's solemn assurances of protection to the wounded, were left a promised sacrifice to the savages, who, immediately after the decampment of the British, entered the house, tomahawked a few, searched all, and then set fire to the house, whirling in their war dance around its flames, and drowning the shrieks of the human victims with their yells. Horrid as this picture is, the present occasion does not allow me to give it a just amplitude and I suppress many incidents which would accumulate horror upon horror. Many of the prisoners which the British drove towards Malden never arrived there, but were murdered by drunken Indians along the way. A hundred instances of the most shocking barbarity occurred at Fort Malden. One of these I will relate.

Captain Nathaniel Hart of Lexington, Kentucky, who commanded a volunteer company from that town, was one of the wounded prisoners taken at Raisin. It happened that the second officer in the British army was a Major Elliott, who many years before had been on the most intimate terms with him, had visited Lexington, lived with Hart almost as his brother for something like a year, and used the house, servants, horses, and purse of old Mr. Hart, with the same freedom that his son Nathaniel had. Poor Hart finding himself a prisoner to Indians, sent for Elliott, gave him his purse of gold for safety, and received a promise of immediate interference in his behalf. Elliott rode off, betrayed his friend to the Indians' knife, and when Hart's murder became notorious, did not scruple to use his money. This case is, to confess the truth, one of the worst that occurred; but there are many which do not fall very far short of it.

General Winchester's division was composed of volunteers from the most responsible classes of society whose homes were chiefly in that part of the State in which Frankfort is situated. Wealthy farmers, lawyers, physicians, ministers of the gospel, distinguished political men, and many very young men of the first families in the State, composed this division—the news of whose massacre, to use Gen. Harrison's expression, overwhelmed Kentucky in tears. Never were the feelings of any people so lacerated. The whole population was clothed in black, and every voice was that of grief.

But in the bosom of a brave and warlike people, grief caused by such inhuman outrages, would naturally subside into a feeling of revenge; (for saints themselves, under such circumstances, would have felt it,) which was cherished and inflamed by the daily intelligence of individual sufferings and fresh barbarities, until the Governor beheld the people of Kentucky ready to turn out en masse, to avenge the cruelties inflicted upon their countrymen. But the British did not permit the excitement from the Raisin affair and its sequels to subside. They repeated at Fort Meigs their cruel indulgence to the Indians, and many of the relatives and friends of the subjects of the former massacre, shared a like fate.

At length Gov. Shelby led a body of Kentuckians to join the North Western army under the command of Gen. Harrison. After our victory on Lake Erie, this army crossed into Canada. That British army which had figured at Frenchtown and Fort Meigs, now fled before the outraged and excited Kentuckians; but they were overtaken at the river Thames, defeated, and many of their officers and soldiers made prisoners. Proctor and the wretched Elliott had outstript all pursuit, and were not of the number. Yet the Kentuckians had now in their possession many of the officers of that army which had violated every thing held sacred in warfare between civilized people, in suffering the most horrid cruelties upon their fathers, sons, brothers, and friends, when they had surrendered upon the most solemn assurances that the articles of their capitulation should be observed in good faith. What was to be expected from the Kentuckians? Men whose bosoms were then bleeding at the dreaded remembrance of a violated capitulation of war, by these very officers, their prisoners. What did the Kentuckians? They treated their prisoners as brave and good men treat prisoners—conducted them in safety and without insult. The Indians who accompanied our army were not let loose on unarmed and defenceless men; to massacre the sound and to burn alive the wounded. My heart, even now, sickens at the remembrance of the faithless sacrifices of my countrymen, and I feel astonished that their brothers and their sons while the transactions were fresh, and when reeking from the battle's heat, could look upon these men and not forget that they were prisoners, in remembering that they were officers at Frenchtown and Fort Meigs.

Our army returned by Fort Malden, where they had leisure to look upon the bullock pen, in which the remnant of the Raisin prisoners was impounded. The officers who placed them there were now, in the turn of warfare, prisoners to us, yet had their very comforts consulted.

Many of the Kentuckians, engaged in this expedition, returned home by Frenchtown. There they found the bones of their kindred and friends, strewed over the plains about the deserted town. What must have been the emotions with which they interred their remains, and when could they become forgetful of their ties to them, of their sufferings, of the authors of the infamous sacrifice and of the feelings which the last kind offices paid to their bones, must have created. Many of these troops resided at Frankfort or its neighborhood.—They had arrived at home a short time before the British officers were removed there. Who could have expected from this populace so much moderation as was shewn towards such prisoners. But before we examine the Frankfort transactions. let us devote a few words to the commencement of the British officer's article in which he charges Colonel Campbell, with parading his prisoners through the principal streets of Chillicothe in Ohio, though such a route was at once circuitous and unnecessary, in order to "insult misfortune." The fact is, that they were marched a few squares, through the principal street, which is not very straight, because it takes its direction somewhat from that of the river and that they were necessarily so marched, to arrive at the boat prepared for their transportation. It is very probable, however, that Colonel Campbell's manners were not altogether agreeable to men, who, presuming upon the sacred safety of their situation as prisoners of an enemy faithful to their engagements, indulged in the language and behaviour of hauteur and petulance: when their former barbarity, their recent ill conduct, and the conciliatory treatment which magnanimity had rendered them, called for a different deportment on their part. The gallant and humane Campbell spent his life in relieving, not insulting misfortune. My personal acquaintance with Lieutenant Harrison, makes me perfectly sensible that he deserves all, probably more even, from those prisoners than that which the British officer has said in his favour: and I give him credit for one instance of liberality.

We are now at Frankfort, but the narrative of the few first days which the prisoners spent there in the Penitentiary, offers nothing worthy of notice, except the profound speculation embraced in it, as to the cause of removing the prisoners to Mr. Weisiger's Hotel—namely Buonaparte's reverses in Russia.

The British Officer tells us that he and his companions were quartered at the first hotel in Frankfort; that they had a large (and I can add beautiful) garden for promenade; that they were allowed a sum, which furnished them with every thing desirable for foibles, with servants, washing, etc; that in the event of illness, the sum was doubled; that a citizen of Frankfort advance to them any amount of money which they from time to time desired, upon their "simple bill;" that they received the hospitality of many of the most respectable families in the place, and neighborhood; and that they were permitted, after a short time, to make excursions for many miles distance, without a guard to control or examine their amusements. Could reasonable men require more at the hand of enemies; enemies too, whose brothers they had suffered to be burnt alive, in violation of a capitulation of war; enemies whose hearts had just been opened to their former grief and resentment by the return of some of their fellow citizens from the plains of Raisin. How prudent, mild, and conciliatory one would be apt to think, must have been the deportment of those officers; to have been treated with so much forgiveness and kindness by these aggrieved people. And, is it possible one would be apt to think, that those officers can ever be sufficiently grateful for so much magnanimity shewn to them. I refer to the British officer's own article, for an account of their manner of treating the inhabitants of Frankfort, and I shall exhibit their gratitude, at least that of the author of the article which we are considering, by an examination of the remarks he makes upon the people.

The country people and the huntsmen, when they came to town, usually went once to see the British. Occasionally a hardy son of the woods could not refrain from bestowing a rough expression upon them, when he called up to his mind the doings of Frenchtown; but he would instantly reflect, that they were prisoners, turn upon his heel, and leave them. Sometimes a rough, facetious clown would apply to them such refined epithets as those which the British officer has inserted in his article. And sometimes a merry, thoughtless youth, would quiz the weaker officers, until they themselves perceived it; when they would look a little contemptuously and walk away, or until they became a little irritated when the quizzer would laugh and leave them. So much for staring at the "British Lions."

Our author informs us of his gratification at witnessing biting and gouging matches, which he says are very common at Frankfort, and is so kind as to describe the process of catching the hair, introducing the thumb, and extracting the eye—and in the other branch, of applying the teeth and taking off the nose. The British officer must, like a certain sect have the power of seeing "thoughts, imaginings, and the amusing creations of the brain;" for the assertion, that he ever saw in Frankfort any real transactions of that sort, between parties of flesh and blood, outrages, at least, my remembrance of Frankfort, as much as the Raisin massacre did the feelings of humanity. The allusion which is made, in the particular use of the feet at Frankfort, is so directly the offspring of real observation, that it deserves never to be separated from its associate in the narrative, which shall now hold up its head in his own words: "It is by no means uncommon to see men in these states deprived of portions of their noses"—"and we fell in with a man who had lost not only his nose, but presented a terrific example of this horrible species of combat, in the wild distortion of eyes half wrested from their sockets." How singular it is that I, who have spent some years and travelled a great deal through the western and south-western states should never have found a face without a nose, except where cancer had demolished it, nor have ever fallen in with a terrific example of the horrible combat, in the wild distortion of eyes half-wrested from their sockets. Does our author, in writing such stuff, mean merely, by the exercise of his imagination to make an amusing article, on the basis of a real campaign; or does he design to persuade his countrymen that the western people are so rude that the British officers were justifiable in burning the dogs alive.

On the occasion of the celebration of the anniversary of their master's birthday, the British officers at Frankfort were, I suspect, more loyal than any other of His Majesty's servants, wherever they may have been located, at home or abroad; that is, if loyalty may be measured by noise; for certainly the same number of men never produced a greater or more incessant volume of racket. I lodged that night at Mr. Weisiger's Hotel, and though I was then but a stripling, I remember distinctly towards the close of the evening, they would stand before the windows which overlooked the street, and bawl out not only the most insulting expressions to the crowd of negroes, children and clowns, but often those of the most disgusting nature. Is it strange that a scene like this, in the centre of a peaceful village, should cause some one or two persons of irritable tempers, to think these men should have greater privileges than our own citizens, who would most certainly have been moderated, long below the elevation to which the carousel of the British officers had arrived.

But the extreme indulgence, and the interference of Mr Weisiger in their behalf, is put down to the low consideration of encouraging the waste of wine for the benefit of his pockets. The same occupation in different places, has very different degrees of respectability attached to it and very different persons accordingly pursue it. Mr. Weisiger was one of the oldest, most worthy and wealthy men of the town and had laid these officers under many obligations to him by his liberality and kind deportment to them. Yet after a few years, forget how much is due to this gentleman, one of these officers puts down a kind action in behalf of him and his companions, to a mean selfishness on the part of Mr. W.

Of the ship affair I have no remembrance. It is very possible that the ingenious young gentleman who formed the vessel, may have presented her and her colours to the eye of some clown, in so insulting a manner, as to have drawn him into the room and caused him to throw the bauble out of the window. This would be of a piece with a hundred silly transactions in which some of these officers were principals.

Now comes Mr. James, and his cigar and his stiletto. "His right hand grasped a stiletto or dirk which he held behind his back." Was the man's body transparent, or did the rays from the instrument of death pass around it? And it was in the night time, now there may be a great deal of basis, in this pretty little story of a hair breadth escape; but, if so, Mr. James must answer for himself. I do really believe however that this, like Shakespeare's *Tempest*, is a noble effort of our author's creative genius. But if, as perhaps it may have been, his imagination in this instance played with our author instead of our author with his imagination, it was a scurvy trick of his imagination, in the stillness of the night, to give him such a race, to cause so desperate a bound over the fence, to give his coat tail to uncertain a grasp, to knock down the yard gate posts and all with his body and then to chase him so closely up to his very chamber, bruised as he must have been and affrighted almost to death as he himself witnesseth. If, however, Mr. James be indicted and tried for an intent to kill, I advise his counsel to plead *non compos mentis* for him—for if a strong, active armed man desire to slay a weak, unarmed, timid creature in a situation and at a time too so well calculated for the deed as that aforesaid, he must be deranged not to have effected his object.

The following handsome affair, is told in an honest version of the British officer's own account.

The British officers, after a general exchange of prisoners, leave Frankfort, under the charge of the Kentucky Marshal, Col. Crocket, who arrives with them at Cincinnati, in Ohio, on the evening of a ball, and they are lodged at the Hotel in which the ball is given. The British officers immediately set about making a noise sufficient to disturb the ladies, in which, by the assistance of wine and songs, they succeed. A gentleman waits upon them and desires that they will moderate the tones of their felicity; he is answered so rudely as to draw upon him something like a threat. But the British officers say to him "we are in your power," and he instantly withdraws, disdaining a contest even in words with men so situated. Col. Crocket, an old revolutionary soldier, whose bosom overran with kindness to every living creature, desire those boisterous gentlemen not to disturb the ladies. A gallant and gallant officer, insults him so very rudely and manifests so strong a determination to continue the disturbance of the party in the ball room, that the marshal is compelled to put him in confinement until morning, when the prisoners bid adieu to the last Kentuckian with whom they had any concern. R.

Letter to the Editor.

TO THE EDITOR OF *THE NEW MONTHLY MAGAZINE.*

SIR,—In "The Philadelphia National Gazette" of the 6th. of August an article has appeared, the tendency of which is to invalidate statements in my "Canadian Campaign." I now notice it only because I am anxious to clear my narrative from the charge of falsehood before the liberal and enlightened part of the American nation, as well as before Englishmen.

This writer, unable to deny the hostile feeling evinced by the Kentuckians and others during our imprisonment, seeks to justify it; and with this view the old and hackneyed story, of American prisoners being handed over to the Indians by British officers for the purpose of being slaughtered in cold blood, is again raked up. Now, it must be borne in mind that this writer says he was, at the time he speaks of, but a mere stripling: how far competent, therefore, to have arrived at an accurate knowledge of the events of the war the reader must determine for himself. No doubt, many of the discomfited backwoodsmen of Kentucky, on their return to their penates, fired his young brain with monstrous tales of the cruelty of British officers; and on these he has possibly grounded his liberal assertions.

Before reading these observations in reply to the comments of the" stripling," the reader will refer to the article "Canadian Campaign," in the preceding pages of this publication, and keep them in view.

The first affair alluded to is that of the River Raisin, contained in No. 2 of the "Campaign," in which, it is stated, the Americans were opposed to the combined Indian and British forces nearly double their number. The article asserts, that, in consequence of the surprise and capture of General Winchester, prior to the commencement of the action, the command devolved "upon Major Madison, who gave so bloody an encounter to the enemy that he had resolved to draw off his forces, if he failed in the stratagem of demanding a surrender, which he accompanied with a threat of yielding up his prisoners, General Winchester and Colonel Lewis, in event of refusal, to the savages, and with the statement that General Winchester ordered them to surrender." It is farther added, that the instant the enemy had laid down their arms, the "savages were let loose on them, murdering more than half their numbers," &c. Now this statement is false in every part. The force of the Americans was equal, if not superior to our own. General Procter held out no such infamous threat. The prisoners were not butchered after their surrender, nor on the route to Amherstburg. The only troops that suffered were those composing the American right wing, which was broken, and pursued by the Indians across the ice, falling almost unresisting victims. As for the assertion, that General Procter had resolved to withdraw his forces at a moment when victory, even though dearly purchased, was certain, it is too absurd to be noticed. That General Winchester signed the order for the surrender,—though the author of this article would insinuate that it was a ruse practised by ourselves,—I can vouch myself: for at the moment when that officer and his son were brought to the rear by the Wyandots, who had captured them, I had assisted in bearing a wounded brother from the field; and during the few minutes I remained near the spot, I saw the American General write the order in question with a pencil, which was instantly conveyed to General Procter, in a distant part of the field, who, until that moment, had not been apprised of the circumstance of the American commander being in our hands.—That several wounded prisoners were burnt in the block-house has been admitted; the force left for their protection being insufficient to restrain the violence of the savages.

The "stripling" states respecting Captain Hart, that "the second officer in the British service was a Major Elliott, who, many years before, had been on the most intimate terms with him, had visited Lexington, lived with Hart almost as his brother for something like a year, and used the house, servants, horses, and purse of old Hart with the same freedom that his son Nathaniel did. Poor Hart, finding himself a prisoner to Indians, sent for Elliott, gave him his purse of gold for safety, and received a promise of immediate interference in his behalf. Elliott rode off, betrayed his friend to the Indian's knife, and when Hart's murder became notorious, did not scruple to use his money." Unfortunately for the credit of this writer, no such officer as Major Elliott ever existed with our division; consequently this second in command, with whom we are now kindly made acquainted, must have been a creature of the "stripling's" brain. To prove, however, his anxiety to affix an unworthy stain on the British name, I will explain his meaning for him. There was a captain of militia named Elliott, a brother of the American naval captain alluded to in No. 3 of my article, who had formerly resided in Kentucky, and who, I believe, was acquainted with the family of Hart; but this gentleman of course could not have been second officer in the British service! Very conveniently, however, for his purpose, the "stripling" finds in the opening pages of my memoir the name of Colonel Elliott, Superintendent of Indian Affairs; and an individual in no way connected or related to the other, and on this gentleman he seems to fasten with an earnestness proportioned to his thirst for denunciation, although Colonel Elliott never knew the Harts, nor was ever in Lexington or the state of Kentucky in his life!

The charge, however, is evidently made against him who had formerly been known to Captain Hart. What the relations were which existed between that unfortunate gentleman and Captain Elliott I know not; but this I do know, that although Captain Elliott was engaged in the affair of Frenchtown, he knew no more than I did that such a person as

Captain Hart was present in the American lines; neither could the sufferer himself have been apprised that the individual who is stated to have been on terms of intimacy with him at an anterior period, was present with our division. But the best proof of the falsehood of this story is, that Captain Hart was one of those who perished in the block-house, of whom I believe none escaped to tell their lamentable tale. When the army returned with their prisoners to Amherstburg, Captain Elliott followed with his company of militia, and was not among those left for the protection of the wounded. So much for this charge.

Again, speaking of the affair on the Miami, detailed in No. 2 of the "Campaign," the American article resumes its charge of cruelty.

> "But the British did not permit the excitement from the Raisin affair and its sequels to subside. They repeated at Fort Meigs their cruel indulgence to the Indians, and many of the relatives and friends of the former massacre shared a like fate."

I appeal to any impartial reader, be he American or Englishman, to say whether after the detailed account I have given of that action, such a charge is honourable. The massacre at the Miami was the only one ever perpetrated in the presence of our troops;[5] and it has been seen that on that occasion, not only the escort sent to convey the prisoners to the gunboats, used every exertion to repel the cowardly attack made by the savages, but that one soldier was shot dead in defending an American victim! Tecumseh himself, fired with a noble indignation at the treachery of their conduct, threatened them with the effects of a vengeance which, but for their instant obedience to his commands, they would have found him not slow to inflict. The escort did all that their strength would allow, while attempting to save their prisoners; had they gone farther and killed any of the savages such an act would have been the signal of destruction of themselves. The writer may tax us with want of ability to restrain the Indians, too much disposed to commit excesses

---

[5] That of the American prisoners sacrificed to the manes of Logan, the Indian chief, at Brownstown, as related in No. 1 of the campaign alone excepted.

of this horrible description. But when he charges us with "granting indulgences," and "giving up prisoners to be tortured and slain," he utters a foul slander.

It is observed, after the affair at the Moraviantown, "our army returned by Fort Malden, where they had leisure to look upon the bullock-pen in which the remnant of the Raisin prisoners was impounded." What this Kentuckian is pleased to call the remnant of the Raisin prisoners consisted of about four hundred and fifty men, the whole of the number who had laid down their arms, though the writer would fain persuade us that one-half had been butchered at the moment of their surrender. His bullock-pen was a large clean space strongly enclosed, and never was used but as a wood-yard for the garrison. No other place, uniting accommodation with security, could be procured; nor could the prisoners have reason to complain, as it was only a place of temporary confinement used during the very few days which preceded their removal to Lower Canada. General Winchester, his son (a fine and amiable youth), and Colonel Lewis, lodged at the principal hotel, and were, I believe, treated with every respect and attention. This much I can say for myself. Being apprised that the two former had lost all their baggage, I had a change of linen and a black silk handkerchief conveyed to each, which trifling articles were politely and thankfully received. Colonel Lewis in return requested me to accept a brace of valuable pistols, in testimony of his sense of the attention I had paid them; but they tend to prove at least that the American prisoners were not treated with harshness.

It is by no means the least amusing thing to find how earnestly this writer descants on the gratitude we should have felt at being permitted to wear our heads on our shoulders. "How prudent, mild and conciliatory (he remarks) one would be apt to think must have been the deportment of those officers: to have been treated with so much forgiveness and kindness by these aggrieved people', and is it possible, one would also be apt to. think, that these officers can ever be sufficiently grateful for so much magnanimity shown to them'?" What a crime, in truth, that we did not bow, and, fawn, and cringe, and thank his countrymen for the boon of life—a boon which by the way would not long have been extended had the sentence of the Queenston deserters been carried into execution. In allusion to the charge against Colonel Campbell of parading us through the principal streets of Chillicothe in Ohio, although such a route was at once circuitous and unnecessary, he observes: "The fact is, that they were marched a few squares through the principal street, which is not very straight, because it takes its direction somewhat from that of the river; and that they were necessarily so marched to arrive at the boat prepared for their transportation. It is very probable, however, that Colonel Campbell's manners were not altogether agreeable to men, who, presuming upon the sacred safety of their situation as prisoners of an enemy faithful to its engagements, indulged in the language and behaviour of hauteur and petulance," &c.

What the writer means by a few squares I know not; the term, like his meaning, is, perhaps, peculiarly his own; but when he denies that we were marched through the streets not immediately conducting to the river, he states that which is absolutely incorrect. We had been sufficiently long in Chillicothe to know every street in the town, and, not having had our eyes bandaged in addition to the handcuffs which lacerated our wrists, had full leisure to survey the nature of our route, which, even by the admission of several American gentlemen, was unnecessarily circuitous. Possibly Colonel Campbell, whose life, we are told, was passed in relieving, not insulting misfortune, took this opportunity of revenging himself for the letters which taxed him, in no very equivocal terms, with the absence of that much vaunted "humanity," which might have been extended without inconvenience to himself, or danger to his government.

“We are now," continues this writer, "at Frankfort, but the narrative of the few first days which the prisoners spent there in the Penitentiary, offers nothing worthy of notice except the profound speculation embraced in it, as to the cause of removing the prisoners to Mr. Weisiger's hotel, namely, Bonaparte’s reverses in Russia." That this is rather a sore subject must he admitted, neither can we feel surprised at the pique evidently manifested by the "stripling" at this passage in the memoir. That Napoleon's unexpected defeat in Russia had given rise to the change in our position, we were assured by several American gentlemen of respectability, was the case; and it certainly must at least he admitted to be a singular coincidence, that our partial liberation should have been ordered immediately after the intelligence of that event reached the seat of Government in America.

Much stress is laid by the "stripling" on the accommodation afforded us at Weisiger's hotel in Frankfort; and he seizes with eagerness on the acknowledgement made in the course of my narrative, that our table was always abundantly supplied, that our bills were liberally cashed, from time to time, by a citizen of Frankfort, and that we experienced the hospitality of some of the most respectable families in the town. These admissions are selected as charges against ourselves, and a sweeping clause of ingratitude is in consequence preferred against us without mercy. That the noble and disinterested conduct of Mr. Sproule, the Frankfort banker, and the kindness and attention paid us by some of the more respectable residents in the place can never be forgotten by those who experienced their influence, no man of proper feeling will for an instant doubt; yet how far these considerations should have entailed any obligation of gratitude to the mass of the rabble, by whom we were, both individually and collectively, insulted on every occasion, I am yet to learn. A for the supplies of our table, they were plentiful, not because the sum allowed us was unusually liberal, but because provisions of every description were cheap, and because the number of officers lodged in the establishment was such as to ensure a certain profit to the innkeeper. The American officers, prisoners in the Canadas, received the same allowance; and if they did not fare quite so well as we did, it was in consequence of the scarcity and dearness of provisions in those provinces. It is far from my intention to charge the American Government with illiberality in our treatment, as far as regarded our animal wants, but certainly it is nonsensical to tax us with ingratitude to that government, as if mere indulgence was given us as officers prisoners of War, than we should have received in France! As far as regards the mass of that state in which we were so uniformly insulted (proverbial for savage manners in all the other states of America) this charge is perfectly ludicrous.

The "stripling" does not relish the Kentuckian phrases inserted in the Memoir; or, as he expresses it, "the refined epithets which the British officer has inserted in his article." I know not whether it be his intention to deny the existence or usage of those phrases in Kentucky, but I believe they are very tolerably impressed on the minds of my brother officers. I charged them only on the State in which I heard them. If, however, he has any doubt on the subject, I will endeavour to remove it by communicating a favourite one of Captain Bradford, who escorted us from Sandusky to Chillicothe, and who subsequently rendered himself conspicuous as an officer of artillery, under General Jackson, in his wars against the Creek Indians. This officer frequently on our route would appear as if awaking from a deep reverie, and, reining in his horse, suddenly turn towards us, exclaiming in a deep and measured tone of voice, "May the Lord J— C—, in the plenitude of his glory, morally, religiously, philosophically, and constitutionally d— my soul to H—," if such or such is not the case. Although fourteen years have elapsed since that period, this extraordinary expression has been too deeply rooted in my memory ever to be forgotten.

Such is the simplicity of the "stripling," that he cannot distinguish between serious assertion and irony; and he evidently chuckles at the discovery he has made of our "gratification" in witnessing "biting and gouging matches," though with unexampled modesty he denies the existence of such practices. I only charge the Kentuckian rabble with what the Americans of other states charge them also: God forbid I should apply my remarks to America generally! In the "Navigator," printed at Pittsburgh on the Ohio, in 1814, in noticing an island called "Battle Island," the work says it was so called from a battle of two Kentuckian bargemen, who went on shore there to decide a quarrel by "rough and tumble." In the contest the cry of "gouging" was heard from the undermost, and they were parted with a "gouge" from one, and a "bite" from the other. Ask the citizens of New York about them. Nay, the foregoing work says, that the Kentuckian is detested on the banks of the Mississippi, and all the planters' doors shut against them. Even the respectable people of that state suffer many inconveniences when travelling in neighboring states. If known to be Kentuckians, they must camp out! p.307. So much for the Kentuckian's "stripling's" sensitiveness—so much for the practice of "gouging" there. From an eyewitness too!—I can assure him, notwithstanding the "outrage to his remembrance of Frankfort," that, without being gifted with the power of seeing "thoughts, imaginings, and the amusing creations of the brain," we had, as I have before asserted, two several opportunities of witnessing a conflict of this description, from the walls of the garden in which we were confined, although the parties were, in both instances, separated in time to prevent any material injury being inflicted.

The "stripling" wilfully distorts one essential passage in relation to this subject, by disingenuously quoting it as applicable to Frankfort, when it extends to two western states. And had he as much candour as prejudice, he would admit that the hatred of any thing English is not more familiar to him than the term "biting and gouging match," with the addition of another word, which must be nameless.

The conduct of the British officers at Mr. Weisiger's, as described by this writer, merits no reply, This person was paid for every thing which we received, as any other tavern-keeper would have been. Obligation we owe him none. In one instance we received an insult from him. Our relations with him were mere matters of pounds and shillings and pence. Of the destruction of the midshipman's vessel this writer recollects nothing. He stopped at the hotel the night before, and has a perfect recollection of our drawing the anger of the crowd upon our heads by our boisterous mirth; but of the attack, not of one clown, but some fifty Frankfort citizens on the Lilliputian vessel, he knows nothing whatever. In truth, we can scarcely blame him for denying all knowledge of the circumstance; for it must be truly humiliating (even to him) to admit the fact of such brutal and unwarrantable conduct.

"Now," continues the article, "comes Mr. James, and his segar, and his stiletto." Was the man's body transparent, or did the rays from the instrument of death pass around it? How very facetious is our "stripling;" but yet, in spite of all his surprising wit, I fear he will find some difficulty in denying this attempt at assassination made by his fellow Kentuckian. Most unfortunately for him, this same Frankfort has been notorious for more than one attempt of the kind. The affair of Beauchamp and Colonel

Sharpe is yet fresh in the recollection of the public; and it was the identical hotel of Mr. Weisiger that the foul assassin selected for his temporary abode, on his arrival to execute his diabolical purpose. There is an evident exultation over the admission, made in the narrative, of an English officer fleeing, to avoid the steel of a cowardly assassin; and on this occasion it is observed, that, if "Mr. James be indicted and tried for an intent to kill, I advise his counsel to plead *non compos mentis* for him —for if a strong, active, armed man desires to slay a weak, unarmed, timid creature, in a situation and at a time so well calculated for the deed as that aforesaid, he must be deranged not to have effected his object." Flight indeed, under every circumstance of the case, was the only chance of escape left for an unarmed youth of sixteen, from such a powerful desperado as Mr. James; and although our "stripling" exhibits all the pettiness of party triumph in alluding to that flight, I am by no means disposed to recall my former confession of the personal dread in which I continued of this assassin until my final departure from Frankfort.

The American article closes with a lame contradiction of the conduct of Colonel Crocket, "an old revolutionary soldier," we are told, "whose bosom overran with kindness to every living creature." If the heart or Colonel Crocket ever overran with kindness, it must have been towards his own countrymen; for in every individual instance, as far as regarded ourselves, we were subjected to all the caprice and insolence of this petty despot. To us he ever behaved with unkindness and tyranny, and certainly we may he permitted to speak of him as we found him.

Throughout the whole of this article there is an evident intention to establish two points: the first is, that the Americans were not only justified in treating us as they did, but that, after the conduct imputed to the officers of our division, we had no right to expect the slightest mercy at their hands, much less to complain of our position: the second is, a sweeping charge of ingratitude against us for presuming to complain or inveigh against the unnecessarily rigid measures pursued towards us, and the insults we experienced from the mass of the Western population. That the assertion made in the opening paragraph is utterly false and ridiculous, not only appears from my own showing, but may be confirmed by many respectable officers who were present with the right division during the whole of the war: and of these I will cite Major-General St. George, and Lieutenant-Colonels Warburton, Chambers, and Hailes, now commanding the 85th, 41st and 28th regiments.[6] The testimony of these gentlemen will certainly weigh more forcibly with every liberal mind, than mere assertions founded in ignorance and nourished by illiberality. As for the charge of ingratitude, let the Americans themselves decide whether I have recorded one instance of personal kindness or gentlemanly demeanor in the whole course of my narrative without rendering every justice to the several individuals by whom that kindness was tendered, or that gentlemanly deportment evinced. As far as I can recollect, I have spoken in the highest terms of the following individuals—of some in a private, and some in a military character—General Harrison, Colonel Croghan, Major Madison, Mr. Sproule, Mr. Brush, Lieutenant Harrison, and Mr. Steele, the Marshal of Ohio. If the "stripling" could name any other individual to whom we have shown ourselves wanting in gratitude for personal obligation, I shall be most happy to acknowledge the omission; but it must be clearly understood, that among this number we do not include either the "humane" Colonel Campbell, the "worthy" Mr. Weisiger, or the revolutionary Colonel Crocket, "whose bosom overran with kindness to every living creature." I believe I may venture to assert, and in the name of my companions in captivity, that neither time nor circumstance can weaken their sense of gentlemanly conduct experienced at the hands of the former gentlemen: but it cannot be reasonably expected that while we pay the debt of gratitude to these individuals, we should overlook the harshness and insults of the majority. When I commenced writing my "Canadian Campaign," it was with a full determination to state such facts only as could readily find confirmation in the testimony of my brother officers, for such alone I conceived admissible into the pages of narrative, professing to detail matter both of a public and private nature. At the same time, while strictly fulfilling both the duty of the historian, and gratifying my own private feelings in rendering a tribute to every American gentleman who had treated us with kindness and attention, I

---

[6] The three latter officers were prisoners of war in Frankfort at the period alluded to.

by no means felt myself called upon to suppress those circumstances which tended to exhibit others in a very different light. Had I been unjust in one instance, I might have been so in all; but I leave it to every impartial American to decide whether we have shown ourselves deficient in proper feeling, where service had actually been conferred; or whether, where such a distinction is made, there must have existed causes for reprobation on the one hand as powerful as those for commendation on the other. My "Campaign" does not possibly please the eye of every American; but although it may contain matter offensive in its sincerity to individuals of that nation, something more than a mere denial of several of its statements, unsupported by proof, and opposed to the united testimony of twenty British officers, must be necessary to shake its claim to consideration on the score of accuracy and fidelity.

RECOLLECTIONS OF THE WEST INDIES

(From the contents as well as the dates of these loose notes, it will be seen that they were thrown together long before the Question of Emancipation became a leading subject of remark and interest in England.)

No. 1

In the Autumn of 1816 the 61st Regiment having been ordered to Jamaica, detachments for the several other corps then stationed in the West Indies were also desired to hold themselves in readiness for embarkation in the same fleet. An officer and forty men of my own Regiment, were soon afterwards marched from Newport Barracks in the Isle of Wight to Cowles where a transport was then lying to receive us. The troops and baggage being received on board, the vessel weighed anchor and returned to Spithead, where she had left the body of the main fleet, completing the preparatory arrangements.

During the time we lay at Spithead, the Russian Frigate conveying the horses sent by their Emperor Alexander to His Royal Highness the Prince Regent arrived, and we had an opportunity of visiting this fine vessel, on board which we were received by the officers, with truly French courtesy and politeness. They were all young noblemen of the first families, attached to the Imperial Guard and wearing several decorations. After having been conducted between decks where the horses were stowed, and examined the dress, arms, and carriage of the men—fine tall athletic looking fellows, and evidently selected for the purpose, we followed our hosts to the cabin where refreshments had in the interim been prepared. The language we used was French, in the knowledge of which however, we betrayed an evident inferiority, as in fact all Englishmen do when placed in competition with Russians of rank and acquirements.—Among the several things placed on the table was the caviar, of which the Russians are known to be extremely fond. Seduced by the tempting appearance of this filthy stuff, I took a large quantity of it in my mouth but sickened and disgusted with the taste, it was in vain that I attempted to swallow it—I was literally in agony, for I could not without a breach of politeness, openly evince the loathing I entertained for a food which the Russian officers devoured with no ordinary voracity and which has since become one of the dishes par excellence in this country, neither could I conquer my repugnance so far as to "bolt" it. Unable to endure this state of torment longer, I rushed upon the deck, much to the surprise of the strangers, and after having committed the caviar to its native element, I returned to the cabin fully resolved never again to indulge to the full extent of a Russian lunch. We soon afterwards took our leave and descended into our boats, assisted by the officers who all stood grouped around the gangway, their full and martial band striking up "God Save the King" in compliment to our party.

Every thing being now ready for our voyage, we weighed anchor from Spithead towards the close of the month, and bearing through the Needles, soon found ourselves fast issuing from the channel. The wind had hitherto been favorable and unabated, but when we entered the horrid Bay of Biscay, it suddenly lulled, and here we were exposed to the dreadful and everlasting roll of this tormenting sea. Who that has ever been in the Bay of Biscay during a calm, can recall without loathing the horrid nausea, and wretched and comfortless state, both of mind and body, incident to such a situation—not to mention the crash and confusion occasioned in the cabin by the unceasing motion of the vessel, rolling her yards, and sometimes even her gunwales, into the troubled deep, while the loose and extended sails, striking with fury against the masts, seem like so many harpies flapping their wings in mockery of your misery and despair. Grant ye Fates that it may never again be my lot to cross the Bay of Biscay. The worst of human ills, however, have their termination. This vile sea was at length passed, and we were glad to admit, that even on the distant waves of the Atlantic, an amelioration of human suffering may be found.

On board the transport in which I was embarked, there were many sick, but neither Surgeon nor medicines had fallen to our share in the distribution. This was an inconvenience severely felt, but eventually supplied by an officer of the 61st, who, with a care and attention which could not have been exceeded by any medical team in the service, administered to their several cases, and, in most instances, with success. During a calm of some hours continuance he had been able to procure a few medicines from the head-quarter ship and these were appropriated to their respective peers, with a skill and anticipation of their effects which would not have disgraced the oldest and ablest practicioner. The severest trial of his judgment and patience was as attention which could not have been exceeded by any medical man in the service, administered to their several cases, and, in most instances, with success. During a calm of some hours continuance he had been able to procure a few medicines from the head-quarter ship, and these were appropriated to their respective uses, with a skill and anticipation of their effects which would not have disgraced the oldest and ablest practicioner. The severest trial of his judgment and patience was a female, the wife of my servant. This young woman had been some time suffering from a cancer in her breast, which from recent neglect has assumed an alarming appearance, at the moment when Lieutenant C— undertook to supply the absence of a regular medical attendant. His attention was now principally devoted to this poor sufferer, and not withstanding the unpleasant exhalation arriving from a wound, to which he never devoted less than half an hour both morning and evening, and in so close a situation as that between decks, he never once shrank from the self-imposed task, and was finally rewarded in the conviction that he had wrought a favourable change in the disease.—Of this I am aware, that although his patient fell a victim to fever shortly after our arrival in Barbados, her breast had some time in a state of convalescence. I have mentioned this circumstance because I conceive it but fair to render testimony to the excellent heart and feelings of a man who without any other prospect than much trouble and responsibility, thus generally undertook what few other officers would under similar circumstances, from a dislike to make the sacrifice of their immediate comfort and ease, and although there was not a single officer on board the transport who did not fully applaud and esteem him for his conduct, there was also perhaps not one who would have profited by the example, or made that conduct his guide—-neither was his care and attention confined to the seriously ill. During our tossing in the Bay of

Biscay, and for some days subsequent, most of the officers were compelled to keep their beds, where they were visited by the new surgeon, not with senna, rhubarb and black draughts but with such delicious, mulled wine, as would have stayed the spirit of one struggling in his last agony.—Sad execution was made with the wine during this period, and such as threatened a speedy annihilation of our stock, but like true soldiers, we thought not of tomorrow while there was a probability of obtaining any thing today, and although our more prudent friend frequently hinted at the fact, as he handed the generous beverage around, such medicine from such hands was not to be rejected.

After having committed the body of a soldier to the deep with the ceremony, or, more properly speaking, want of economy usual on such occasions at sea, we came within sight of the Island of Madeira, which much to our regret we passed without stopping, although the full and distinct view obtained of the white and dazzling edifices of Fanchal proclaimed our little squadron to be at no great distance from that place. The disappointment of the Officers of our transport was great indeed, for we had fully calculated on repairing at Madeira the serious breach which had been so very imprudently made in our wine cellar. But after having long and vainly watched for some propitious signal from the Agent-Commodore who pursued his course past this Bachus-favor'd port, with a steadiness indicative of no want of incense to sacrifice to the Deity himself, we were compelled to call in the aid of philosophy, and consent to a reduction in our daily consumption.

As we crossed the line the usual filthy and disgusting operation of shaving was practised on the younger and more untravelled portion of the men, who in many instances proved refractory, and in some inflicted severe chastisement on the brutal Neptune and his satellites. From a conviction that the practice tends in a great degree to the subversion of military discipline, I had decidedly opposed the thing from the commencement, but as there was an officer senior to myself on board as decidedly in favor of the ceremony, I was, of course compelled to submit to his decision. A plot had in the interim been formed by a part of the crew, at the head of which was the carpenter who personated Neptune, the object of which was to not only force me but Lieutenant M

—of my Regiment, who had been equally hostile to the measure, to undergo the customary shaving and ablution.—Of this however we were apprized in time, when disgusted and enraged by so much insolence, we loaded our pistols and intimated to the Master that if any of his crew dared to lay hands on us we should shoot them without hesitation on the spot. This threat, which by the way, would not have proved a mere threat, had they proceeded to extremities, had the desired effect, and the affair passed off without other incidents, than those produced by the application of some heavy and well directed blows from the infuriated men on their tormentors. Not was it without deep exultation that I beheld the filthy God himself prostrated on the deck by a blow from the vigorous arm of one of the men of my detachment, the instant he was liberated from the ordeal. The vessel on this day presented the highest possible scene of confusion. Every thing like order and discipline were at an end, and the officers were obliged to mount half naked into the highest part of the rigging, in order to escape the deluge of water poured from the main yards and shrouds on the deck, and inundating even many parts of the cabin. With these consequences of the observance of a foolish and ridiculous custom, it can only be a source of surprise that officers either in command of the Regiments or Detachments should suffer the continuance of a practice which is, I maintain, subversive, at least for a time, of that good order and discipline which should at no moment suffer the slightest relaxation or diminution.

No. 2

The moment of my arrival at Barbados proved to be inauspicious and unfavorable. The yellow fever had been some time raging in the Island and not only the troops but the Inhabitants had suffered from this cruel and devastating scourge. Among the first of its victims was the Commander in Chief Sir Charles Leith, who had been interred only a short time previous to our arrival. The sudden demise of this gallant Officer had thrown a shade of melancholy on every brow, and in every circle the deep and unqualified regret occasioned by his untimely fate, was the theme of conversation. The mild administration of his Government, and his many eminent private virtues had rendered Sir James Leith no less a favorite with the Inhabitants of Barbados, than with the troops, a part of whom having served with him in the Peninsula, and marked his high bearing in the hour of danger and of victory, were fully competent to appreciate his distinguished qualities as a soldier.

Death had not been idle in my regiment. Several officers and many men had perished, and on the day of my arrival, all left the mess-table at an early hour to follow one of their associates to the grave. That evening, two others were carried to the hospital in a state of feverish madness, and one having been seized with the "black vomit," was, on the following day, a corpse. Such were the heart-rending scenes that frequently occurred during the prevalence of this disorder and the soul sickened with disgust for a country where, at one moment you beheld the friend of your bosom—the companion of many years and many scenes—the sharer of your privations, your dangers, your glories in the field, seated at the festive board, in the full enjoyment of health and strength, and gaiety of heart, and in the next, suffering from an accumulation of torment which has no example, while a few short hours alone were necessary to waste him to more than infant weakness, and sever the slight thread which bound him to existence.

I cannot better exemplify or describe the progress of the sensations attendant on this malady, than by a detail of an attack which I experienced about ten days after my arrival on the Island. Anxious, as most young men usually are, to see whatever is to be seen in a new country, immediately after a long sea voyage, and heedless of all prudential admonitions to the contrary, my friend M—and myself frequently indulged in visits to the town during the intense heat of the day. The distance from the barracks was nearly a mile, and, exposed to the scorching rays of a sun to whose effects we were not yet sufficiently inured, it cannot excite wonder that we should thus have inflamed and predisposed our blood to the active influence of miasma. I had suffered much during the last few days from violent lumbago, yet on the morning of the attack, I felt otherwise perfectly well. I had been one of the Officers of the main guard on the preceding day, and was now in the very act of being relieved when the blood suddenly rushing with great violence to my head, caused it to ache with intenseness, and it was not without extreme difficulty, that, supported by my sword, I contrived to reach my barrack room, distant about sixty yards. On entering my apartment, I had only strength sufficient to throw myself on my bed, when the most cruel delirium succeeded. My servant, who had hastened instantly for assistance soon returned with the Assistant Surgeon, attended by two men with a litter. On this I was immediately placed, and conducted to the Hospital, and, having been placed in bed, submitted to the operation of the lancet. Both temporal arteries were opened, and every drop of blood, that could well be got at, was taken away. This, of course, relieved my brain from the suffocating weight with which it had been oppressed, but left my whole system in a state of extreme debility. My sensations, which had hitherto been those of violent and irritable pain, were now those of calm and almost disregarded suffering, yet the disease continued to undermine, and when visited on the following day by the medical staff of the Garrison, I was wasted to a skeleton, and deprived of the power of speech, although not insensible. Little deeming, I presume, that I understood a word they said; they after some slight conversation in regard to my situation, expressed their decided opinion, that nothing more could be done for me. I have never thought of inquiring of those who have recovered from an equal low state of suffering with myself and produced from the same fever. whether they entertained a similar and total indifference to life, and consequently ascertaining whether that indifference is a result or effect of this particular disorder. But I perfectly recollect that although convinced the prediction of my medical attendants would not be verified, not the slightest anxiety for the result ever once stole across my mind, and if I experienced any thing like regret, it was from the sad feeling of loneliness attached to the idea of terminating my earthly career on a distant and inhospitable shore.

At this moment of this visit I was in a state of utter exhaustion, and life appeared to have entirely forsaken my lower extremities. More than once I essayed to raise my legs with my hands but they fell like a dead weight from my grasp, and were cold as marble. It certainly was a singular situation to be placed in, and the idea of a supposed dying man coolly taking up his limbs in succession as he felt the hand of death stealing gradually over him, might at any other moment, have called up a smile even, on his own emaciated countenance. At length the disorder, equally worn out with myself, ceased to rage, and I gradually and slowly recovered my strength.—On the following day I heard the voice of my poor friend M—who had followed me almost immediately to the hospital and had been placed in the adjoining room. His accent and language were those of tearful delirium, and I was so much effected in consequence that I begged the Assistant Surgeon to cause one of us to be removed to a more distant apartment. This he promised and soon afterwards I was informed that my friend had been taken away. The next day I was so much recovered as to feel a desire to read, and I despatched one of my attendants to the Hospital-Assistant for a book. He soon returned, not with a book, but with the *Barbados Mercury* of that morning. The paper was folded, and in such a way, that my glance fell first on the column containing the deaths. My surprise may be imagined on finding that it contained the following announcement "Died yesterday at St. Anns, and was buried this morning, Lieutenant M— of the —regiment" I continued to rivet my eyes on the article with stupid earnestness, yet I believed the statement to be incorrect, for I had been told, only a few hours before that M— was recovering. The Assistant-Surgeon who had give me that assurance, coming in soon afterwards, I silently placed the paper in his hands, watching his countenance as he perused the announcement. There however I could trace no expression of surprise, and finding that concealment was no longer practicable, he observed that the article was too true, and that M—had in reality been buried that morning. The shock this intelligence gave me was sever, and operated not a little to retard my recovery. Poor M—. I little imagined when I heard his powerful accents in the raving of delirium, that that delirium was what it proved to be, the precursor of his death—still less did I conceive, wen informed of his removal from the apartment that this removal had been to the dark and hungry tomb of Barbados.

I now began gradually to recover, and aided by some generous Madeira five and twenty years in bottle, which had been purchased at the sale of Sir James Leith's effects, by the Colonel of my regiment, who distributed it with no sparing hand among the sick and convalescent, was at length enabled to leave the hospital for the barracks—alas, how changed were the number and condition of its inmates.—Of those whom I had so recently left high in health and strength, several were removed where no human eye could ever more behold them, and many presented in their wasted forms and sallow countenances unerring proofs of the suffering by which they had been assailed, nor could a feeling of melancholy be repressed on gazing at the healthy forms of the yet unharmed, who trod as it were on a concealed fire, and might, in the next hour, be cut off from friend and existence for ever. When during my convalescence I was visited by the senior Captain present with the regiment (acting as Commanding officer during a temporary indisposition of the Colonel) and by the Adjutant, both of whom were then in perfect health. After having congratulated me on my evident amendment and conversed about an hour, they took their leave with the expression of a hope that I would soon be enabled to join them at the mess table. Three or four days but succeeded to this visit, when I left the hospital, when on inquiring for these officers, I was told that they reposed in their graves! The picture I have drawn of my own feelings and sufferings is such as may apply to every other patient. Few can understand, like those who have experienced it, the dreadful loathing and dislike, entertained by a sick European, for a climate whose every blast carries pestilence and death to some devoted bosom—and where disease if it does not kill, is sure to tinge the mind with the most depressing melancholy.

Amid all the horrors by which he is surrounded, consequent on this cruel malady, it is however ever a source of much satisfaction to the sufferer to know, that whatever human art and attention can effect in mitigation, he is certain of obtaining. In no country perhaps do military hospitals possess greater advantages than at Barbados. The medical Gentlemen of this establishment are generally of confirmed talent and approved practice, and having, many of them at least, the powerful aid of long experience in a disease which has become their principal study, are thus qualified to inspire a confidence in the patient which is not infrequently of absolute import to the favorable termination of his malady. Much attention is also paid as well to the wards of the men as to the rooms of the officers, which are capacious and clean, and kept constantly ventilated. Independent of the regular attendants attached to the hospital. there are also nurses employed to sit up with the patient, an administer to his wants. These women are generally mulattoes and acquit themselves of their charge with a fidelity, zeal, and watchfulness, which seldom fail to create a strong feeling of gratitude in the breasts of those whom they are often greatly instrumental in restoring. During my illness, one of these kind creatures was my constant attendant, and nothing could induce her to leave me for any length of time.

So many learned and professional men have treated of, and differed from each other in their opinions, in respect to the cause or origin of what i generally termed yellow fever, that it may almost be deemed presumption in me to hazard an opinion on the subject, but there is one circumstance which appears so confirmatory of the idea I have ever entertained, that the yellow, or bilious, fever like the intermittent, is produced by miasma, that I cannot refrain from giving it insertion. At Barbados there are two barracks. The one of stone is situated near the sea—the other of brick, at a distance of about three hundred yards from the first, lies near a hollow or basin near the parade ground which is frequently filled with water that is suffered to become stagnant, and from which the most noxious exhalations sometimes arise. Now it was remarked that every officer residing in the latter barrack was attacked by fever, while not one of those in the opposite building suffered in the least—and as this hollow was filled with water during the continuance of the afflicting malady, it cannot be unreasonable to infer that so partial an influence must have arisen from something more than mere chance, and that circumstances of a local character must have created so wide and extraordinary a distinction. These however are mere facts—I leave it to the faculty to decide on the correctness or incorrectness of the conjectures they elicit—as the fever is however confessedly known to be of a bilious nature, Europeans on going to the West Indies would do well to ready and alter the tone of the stomach by the copious use of calomel, which may be used with effect, and without inconvenience on the passage.

From all that has come under my own personal observation, as well as what I have understood from others on the subject, I am inclined to think that persons of what may be termed "middling constitution," are those who combat most frequently with success against the yellow fever —A very powerful constitution, in the vigorous struggle which it maintains for its mastery with this unpitying scourge, of tropical climates, generally sinks under the violence of its own efforts, while a weakly one is, on the other hand, at once overwhelmed by the overpowering tide of disease acting on blood even to madness. Most of our officers who persisted were men of vigorous forms, and so general was the effect produced on such constitutions that we eventually seldom saw a robust person attacked by the fever without anticipating the most fatal result. My constitution had previously been much tried in America, and by other diseases, and although far from weak, could not be said to be very powerful. Of the officers of the regiment who were attacked about this period, one only beside myself survived, and he subsequently perished.

No 3.

The first destination of a Regiment, on embarking for the West Indies, is (Jamaica excepted) almost invariably Barbados; yet strange to say, the duty of the soldier is, by some capricious regulation, infinitely more severe than is any other Island. One would naturally imagine that, insufficiently inured to the climate, fatigue of every description, should, as far the interests of the service may permit, be spared to the troops. Commandants in Barbados, however, pride themselves much on being strict disciplinarians, and fancy it necessary to drill Regiments into fever, before they can with safety be distributed among the other Islands—a change which is generally effected after a few months continuance at Head Quarters. Independently of the daily morning parades, which might in fact with propriety be termed night parades—the gun signal, arousing both officers and men from their slumbers long before dawn of day—and which are not infrequently continued for several consecutive hours, there are three or four Garrison parade days during the week, when the troops are turned out in heavy marching order under the scorching rays of a post-meridian sun. Sunday however is the day par-excellence, when the troops are arrayed in full dress, and the officers, buttoned up to the throat, with white sword belt and Hessian boots, and light pantaloons, are compelled to rise most unwillingly, from the mess-table, for the purpose of gratifying the curiosity of the indolent inhabitants, who assemble from all quarters to see the Garrison pass in review. Here whites, blacks, mulattos, cobs, mustees, quadroons, and every rank, shade, circumstance, and bearing, are indiscriminately blended—each class looking down on that immediately beneath it, with the most unqualified contempt, from the pale and ghastly looking Creole to the unmixed offspring of the sooty African. The few who have carriages of any description make a point of displaying them on this occasion, and, what with horsemen and pedestrians, contrive to form a dense and motley mass around the saluting post whence they are only to be finally driven, by the band striking up, at the desire of some officer —piqued and fatigued by his recent laborious exertion—the air of "Paltry Badian" a contempt-implying piece of national music, which seldom fails to clear the parade ground.

It is really often ridiculous to observe the extent to which pride of cast is carried in the West Indies, and especially in Barbados—those who approach nearest in complexion to the white, ranking ever first in the scale of comparison. The contempt with which the unfortunate negro is looked upon by the mulatto who is but one shade removed, and must consequently have owed his origin to an African parent, is truly absurd; and would scarcely be credited by those who have never had an opportunity of witnessing its display—"Get out of my way, you black rascal. How dare you speak to me, you black nigger," and many other expressions of a similar nature, I have frequently heard addressed to the unhappy black, who, forgetting the due quantum of respect exacted by these copper-colored gentry, has chanced to intrude himself on their notice, or accost them in the language of familiarity. The contrast in their dispositions is also striking, and may be more especially observed while in a state of voluntary servitude, for although the mulatto considers it highly derogatory to his color and dignity to enter into service, he is often compelled by circumstances to do so and ever makes a disagreeable attendant. Proud and sullen by nature, the moroseness of his disposition is increased by the idea of humiliation which he attaches to his condition, and an unbending frown is usually stamped on his gloomy brow. This feeling is much more forcibly manifested when there are blacks serving immediately with them, for recurring ever, and in bitterness of spirit, to the common stock from which they mutually have sprung, the imaginary distinction is leveled at his own eyes, although he still seeks to impress the servant with whom he is linked, with a high idea of a superiority, which is often only admitted by reason of the comparative state of independence and liberty usually attached to his condition. The free back, on the contrary, entirely exempt from those petty feelings and jealousies by which those above him are tormented, enters with gaiety and pleasure into a service which he can break off at pleasure, and happy in the reflection that he at length possesses that personal liberty for which he has so long sighed, and knows so well how to appreciate when obtained, ever appears both cheerful and contented.

I have invariably remarked, whenever opportunities have been afforded me, that th unhappy slaves are even more harshly treated by people of color than by the whites themselves, and that if possible their labour is rendered even more severe. More than once have I beheld a chain of fettered negroes, both men and women, driven for petty misdemeanors, by some tyrant of a mulatto. Proprietor, who mercilessly applying the searching lash to their back, has seemed to experience a secret delight in their sufferings. No sentiment of compassion could warm the bowels of these unfeeling retches, nor did the recollection that their own mothers had in all probability been placed in a similar situation. and suffered in a similar manner, seem in any one instance to occur to them.

The Barbadians have the affectation to consider themselves out of the West Indies altogether, and whenever a voyage to any other Island is projected or undertaken it is believed “such or such person is gone to the West Indies.” Their own soil they dignify by a no less high-sounding title than that of "Little England." It certainly may be called little England inasmuch as it is an Island, but what the other component parts are which constitute the resemblance, I confess myself so dull as never to have discovered; though they may found their claim to the distinction on the alleged fact of their air being purer—their soil richer—their climate more healthy—and their population more numerous than their neighbors can boast. Another ad no less weighty reason which they assign, is that they possess more luxuries. The only luxury, of which I have remarked them to be exclusively possessed, is that of carriages, which the flat nature of their Island enables them to indulge in, and which are only not common to the country at large because its generally uneven and mountainous character precludes all possibility of their being used, except in a very partial degree.

There is a race course at Barbados, which is usually well attended, and where some tolerably good horses may be seen. On these occasions, the country exhibits an air of liveliness in which it is, at other moments, sadly deficient, for although the assemblages of all that Barbados can boast of vehicles and fashionable display may afford gratification to the fairer portion of society, horse racing is but a secondary amusement to the men, whose attention seems to be devoted exclusively to cock-fighting. In every part and among every class does this exist; and many persons have been known to ruin themselves by their rage for high betting at this barbarous pastime. Even distinction of rank and caste is thrown aside on these occasions, and the usually stern and unbending features of the planter are seen to soften into almost idiotic expression, while awaiting, with intensest interest, the issue of the combat, and watching, its vicissitudes. Cocks are not infrequently introduced on the table with the dessert, and the ringing of broken bottles and crashing of glasses is often blended with the loud shouts and execrations of the guests, as victory is seen to hang over, or desert the bird of their selection.

I was once, while on detachment in the country, invited, with two others of my corps, to dine with a Regiment of Barbadian Militia, the Officers of which were residents in the neighborhood. Curious to know how the mess of a Regiment of Barbadian Militia was conducted, we gladly accepted the invitation and were early in our attendance. After having been introduced severally, and in a somewhat formal manner by the Colonel to his officers, we were ushered into a room adjoining that in which they dined, and much to our astonishment, observed that it was a regular cock-pit, while numerous pairs of spurs, or gaffs, lying about, sufficiently apprized us of the entertainment which was in reserve. The different members of the corps now commenced a dissertation on cock-fighting which to us was unintelligible as Hebrew, and which might have continued for some hours had not the announcement of dinner, diverted for a moment the current of their language, if not of their ideas. I had the honor of being placed on the right hand of the President, who however proved to be the most dull and uninteresting President I had ever met with, and as the conversation soon after we had been seated, resumed its beaten track, and cocks and pits, and gaffs, and bets became the noisy and unceasing theme, we were left half the time to our own reflections, which were certainly not much in favor of our hosts who appeared to have lost sight of all sense of politeness and good breeding in the intemperate ardor of their discussions. We were not a little puzzled moreover in helping our selves to wine, which was placed on the table in a singular and highly forbidding manner. Each member of the mess had a black bottle before him, from the neck of which was suspended a card, on which was inscribed his name, in letters of a size to frighten away the boldest intruder.—When asked to take wine we were literally confused, for none had been placed before us, and when glancing to the right we saw the character "Colonel" or "Major" or "Captain" so and so, defending as it were the property confided to their care, while on the left, as equally formidable array met our enquiring eyes, we knew not well what to do. Our dilemma was certainly good-humoredly and promptly relieved by a dozen owners of black bottles, all offering their wine at the same moment, but this only made the affair more awkward. When we left, half the cock-fighters, from inability to sit at it, were under the table—the others in the pit.

No. 4

The town of Bridgetown, and the capital of Barbados, is situated in a valley near the sea, and is open on several sides to the land breeze, which is sweeping gently along the surface of the more mountainous parts of the Island, falls with refreshing coolness on the town. The selection of vallies for the sites of towns, as is so generally the case in the various West India Islands, can however only be ascribed to commercial considerations, a contiguity to the shipping being ever an object of importance with the inhabitants, or, except during the prevalence of these breezes, which are partial and only of a few hours continuance, the atmosphere is oppressive even up to suffocation, while the rays of the scorching sun, falling on the white road and buildings, dazzle and weaken the eye with their glare. The only protection they have against this is the verandah which, projecting some distance from the house, intercepts the rays of the sun and presents, in its livelier green, a partial relief to the monotonous and offensive white of the buildings. These houses are principally inhabited by shop keepers and tradespeople who, in the numerous conveniences arising from a residence near the sea, appear to lose sight of comforts which have not an immediate tendency to promote their commercial interests, and to fancy the preservation of health a matter of inferior consideration. The more respectable and independent inhabitants reside chiefly in the country, where they enjoy a purity of atmosphere, and breathe with a freedom unknown to those who live in town.

At the southern extremity of Bridgetown, commences a range of wooden buildings of a very secondary character indeed, forming a street about three quarters of a mile in extent, running parallel with the sea and reaching to the Barrack of St Ann's. These are chiefly occupied by mulattoes, and in all, with very few exceptions, may be observed a fondness for ostentatious display which struck me on my arrival as one of the principal characteristics of these people, and which I subsequently found to be common to the West India Islands. Glass is the article of which they appear to be the most fond, and possess in the greatest abundance—Several of these houses, whose furniture exceeded not an old bed, table, and a few crazy chairs, were, notwithstanding, ornamented with a wide side board containing shades, sangree glasses, and various others evidently laid out for the purpose of attracting the admiration of the passenger. It appeared as though many of them had expended all they possessed in the world in the purchase of these articles, for their houses or huts otherwise bore evident marks of the poverty of those by whom they were inhabited.

This range of buildings, I have already remarked is principally occupied by mulattoes and these are for the most part women—yet although many are poor, there are not wanting those who by their consequential air and language, (an invariable criterion by which to discover wealth in this country) prove them to be beyond the reach of the frowns or caprices of fortune. These women contrive to enrich themselves gradually, either by hiring out the few slaves they have as servants to the officers of the Garrison, or by sending them to the barracks, laden with the various fruits and vegetables of the country. Another article of commerce also is the spruce beer, large quantities of which are daily sold among the troops, and, at an early hour in the morning, numerous groups of these vendors, their heads bending under the weight of cocoa nuts, yams, fruits, spruce beer, etc, may be seen advancing to the spot, where, literally melting beneath the intense heat of a vertical sun, they are compelled to remain until a late hour in the evening—Occasionally visited by their pompous mistresses, whose watchful eyes are ever on the alert, these poor creatures have but little time or opportunity for idleness, and thus does the sluggish wheel of their unvaried existence go round. Formidable too is the appearance of these female slave owners, for to a rotundity of form and stateliness of manner which would not disgrace an English Duchess, they unite a severity of countenance which cannot fail to infuse terror into their unfortunate dependents. An immense turban is also one of their constant appendages, and over this, by way of ornament, (certainly not of convenience) a hat is worn, when they go any trifling distance from their homes. The younger and more coquettish of the mulatto women usually wear one with a narrow brim, which can never have the effect of protecting their faces from the sun. The more matronly, on the contrary, arm themselves with one exceedingly broad in the beam—I sue the term "arm" for a hat of this description is no less formidable than a lady's hoop was wont to be at Buckingham House, and with this imposing article of headgear, surmounted by an umbrella, they exhibit a truly grotesque appearance, and strut along as proudly and consequentially as if each considered herself Empress of the world—her head square to the front and as immoveable as that of the Tartar sentinel planted over the Turkish artillery by Baron de Tott. The Mustee women who are much fairer, and whose hair is consequently finer, do not wear this turban, but, on the contrary, are at much pains to show it off to the greatest possible advantage.

The hospitality of the Barbadians has been much cried up to those about to embark for the West Indies, but during the period that we were quartered in Barbados, we did not find that it was exercised except in a very partial degree. In the remoter parts of the Island where our small detachments were occasionally stationed, and among a very few of the more respectable proprietors, the several officers in command did certainly meet with some attention, but this was almost wholly confined to the outposts. With the inhabitants of Bridgetown generally, we had very little intercourse, a strong feeling of dislike existing between themselves and the officers of the garrison—the first actuated by low feelings of jealousy seeking every to annoy the officers while the latter, openly evincing their unqualified contempt for the consequential manners of the "Little Englanders," were but too ready to manifest it on every possible occasion. It might be imagined that men, incurring the peril of blighting disease, for the preservation of the property and lives of individuals from the fury of a host of enslaved and suffering bondsmen, would at least find some compensation for the miseries incident to such a situation, in the kindness and good feeling of those individuals, but such is far from being the case with the Barbadians, whose littleness of pride is, in all probability, aroused by the consciousness of owing their well being and security to strangers, and ingratitude, we all know to be the recompence of services conferred on the low and the groveling of spirit—Could an English officer descend so far as to solicit an introduction into society, he would find no great difficulty in obtaining it, but that becoming pride by which he is ever governed, causes him to recoil from the bare idea of such humiliation, and although it is not of course without violence to his feelings and inclinations that he finds himself deprived to a certain extent of female society, he is far from having the slightest desire to enter into any other, for the officers of a regiment, we well know, form a society in themselves and possess too many internal resources to feel, even in such a country as this, at a loss for amusements unconnected with those in which females partake. There is one custom practiced here which is exceedingly disgusting, and that is the mode of sending invitations, when they do condescend to ask the officers. Without taking the trouble to call previously, or even to send separate cards, a note is usually despatched to the Colonel, authorizing him to bring with him those he may think proper to select—a specimen of politeness which reflects infinite credit on the higher classes of Barbadian society. It is by no means unimportant for the young subaltern, anxious to launch himself into female society on any terms, to rank high in the good graces of his commanding officer on these occasions. Sometimes a card is despatched to the officers collectively, but even this, though less offensive, we used to consider rather too cavalier a mode of invitation, and it was consequently declined by the majority—a few young men only accepting it with a view to gratify their curiosity, and procure introductions to certain fair dames whom they had perhaps encountered as strangers during their rides, and whose images had made a deep impression on their senses, if not on their hearts.

The women of the West Indies are however by no means endowed with those qualities of mind which are so necessary to fix the affection and establish their empire over the hearts their adorers. That rich proportion of form which they possess in no trifling degree, cannot of course fail to enslave the senses, but he who recovering from the trance produced by that style of beauty by which they are in general characterized, would seek mind worthy to animate and ennoble such a form will be sadly disappointed indeed. Shamefully neglected in their education and brought up in idleness and apathy, their conversation is trivial and insipid, and although their eyes would bespeak a mind susceptibly alive to those feelings which owe their being to education and the cultivation of mind, we are soon compelled to confess, that what appeared to be an emanation of soul, is but the action of imagination.

Even in the lighter accomplishment of drawing and music they are in general miserably deficient, and, although the sounds of the piano assail the ears of the passenger through the jalousies of almost every respectable dwelling, they are of such a description, as to induce him to imagine that mediocrity in music, as in all other things, is the point of proficiency beyond which they care not to pass—the *ne plus ultra* of their capability. It does appear extraordinary that in a country where ostentation and display seem to be the regulating principles of the inhabitants, no seminaries of a respectable description should be provided for the education of females, which, if properly attended to, would render them truly delightful members of society—but public institutions of any description are no where to be met with in the West Indies, neither is the slightest encouragement given to the arts and sciences. Satisfied with the accumulation of wealth, the selfish and indolent planter cares not whether the minds of his offspring be brutalized by the same ignorance in which his own speculating term of years has been wrapped, convinced as he is that that ignorance is no barrier to the acquirement of luxurious independence and unbounded gratification. The only women in the Island who can be said to have any accomplishments whatever, are those whose educations have been completed in England, whither many of them are frequently sent for the purpose at an early period of their lives, yet many even of these appear to profit but little by the advantages thus afforded them over the majority of their country women, and it is often necessary to receive an information (which is generally voluntarily given,) to know that they had ever been in England at all. How much pains and expense might be saved with those, and what fascinating creatures might be made of all, were but a small portion of that wealth which is hourly spent in extravagance, appropriated to the formation of a respectable establishment in this Island. Teachers of every description, and of the first abilities would be found ready and willing to engage themselves from home, and in sufficient number to undertake the education of those who, attracted by so advantageous a consideration, would be sent from the various other Islands to swell the size and increase the respectability of the schools.

There was one circumstance which occurred, during our stay in Barbados, and which led us, and perhaps not unjustly, to tax these fair beings with the most disgusting affectation. I had remarked, soon after my recovery from fever, that the funerals, both of Officers and men, were performed without the music usual on these occasions. My surprise was not less when given to understand that this part of the military ceremony had been discontinued at the request of the ladies of Bridgetown who, finding their nerves too weak to bear the dismal strains of the Dead March, had petitioned the Commandant of the Garrison to that effect. This might have been forgiven them had they evinced the slightest consistency, but it was notorious that whenever the funeral of an Officer took place, the balconies of every house along the road which led to the burial ground in the town, were filled with females whose countenances bore any other expression than that of melancholy or sympathy for the dead. The feeling excited among the Officers generally, by the palpable inconsistency of such conduct, was not the most flattering either to the hearts or understandings of the Barbadian fair.

The greatest number of women we ever saw collected together at one time in Barbados, was at a ball given by the President of the Island in honor of her Majesty's birthday. The rooms were brilliantly illuminated, and nearly three hundred ladies, many of them splendidly attired, were present. If the West Indian women are spiritless in all things else, they by no means want grace and animation in the dance—an amusement to which they are decidedly partial. There is a energy about them during these moments which proves to what extent they may be awakened from their apathy. Many of those assembled on this evening, to indulge in their favorite exercise, were extremely beautiful women, and on the whole our gratification as spectators was great. A sumptuous supper had been provided for the occasion, and to a table elegantly disposed and covered with every possible delicacy, the fair dancers repaired, at a late hour. Dancing was renewed after supper, and it was not until daylight in the morning that they quitted the exhilarating scene of gaiety and festivity, to sink again into apathy and indolence until another similar occasion should recall them to life and energy.

At a latter period the routs and conversaziones of Lady Combemere formed a kind of epoch in the history of Barbadian amusements, but these, never very numerously attended, were of too fashionable and nonchalant a character to suit the taste of West Indian ladies generally. Perhaps also many were unwilling to risk a comparison with her Ladyship whose wit, beauty, elegance, and ton were wont to ensure her the palm in the first circles of London Society, and must have rendered any attempt at competition utterly hopeless in the Colonies.

No. 5

For a lover of the picturesque there is little to be found worthy of attention in Barbados scenery, for although the first appearance of the Island as it meets the anxious eye of the voyager willing to find beauty in any thing in the shape of land is favorable and prepossessing, the character it assumes on a more intimate acquaintance, and the impressions it conveys are widely different. Instead of branching firs and oaks rich in the majesty of age, and spreading their luxuriant foliage to the summer breeze, here the tall and thinly covered coca nut tree, with yellow leaves of stubborn texture, arrests the eye on every hand, and present in its sickliness of hue no unfair emblem of the climate which has given it birth, while the palm, with its voluminous and greener leaf, wears that monotonous stillness which gives insipidity to inanimate as to animated nature. I never yet could behold a cocoa-nut tree emerging from its bed of sand, and carrying along its tall and naked trunk, every appearance of barrenness, without indulging in a certain train of melancholy thought. This feeling cannot well be described, but those who have resided in the West Indies for any time, without associating the idea of home with surrounding objects, may fully understand it. At the more northern extremity of Barbados, however, there is some little diversity in the general aspect of the country, which wears a less open character and in some parts abounds with small and lively woods, which have hitherto escaped the axe of the cultivator. The endless range of sugar cane plantations are moreover an additional bar to the existence of beautiful scenery, and as the eye wanders over the general surface of the country, it is every where met by the same character of languid dulness and monotonous fertility. Of the richness of the soil, however there is every proof in the acknowledged fact of many crops of sugar canes being reproduced by themselves from the original stocks and without requiring the slightest trouble from the cultivator. A planter assured me that his estate had produced sixteen crops in successive seasons without the cane being replanted or the soil manured in the slightest manner during this period. This appears almost incredible. The soil however exhausts itself in the course of time and in 1812, that of Barbados had become extremely impoverished, when a novel species of manure was rather miraculously supplied, in a volcanic eruption which took place in a distant Island (St. Vincents.) The several accounts given of this occurrence by eye witnesses were in general alike and exceedingly interesting. About twelve o'clock on the day of the explosion, a dark and dense cloud of matter suddenly appeared over Barbados, and increasing in extent and fulness, soon spread itself over the whole Island, descending gradually and obscuring the light of Heaven. The inhabitants of course were filled with the deepest alarm and astonishment at this unexpected and threatening event, and many fancied that the end of all things was consummating. It soon became dark as night, and hundreds in their despair flew to the churches and passed a few distracted moments at the foot of the altar—Mothers, frantic with dread and grief, sought and clung to their offspring in all the agony of uncertainty. Lights flew rapidly by, indicating by their waking course the desperation and terror of those by whom they were borne, and the most dreadful scenes of confusion were every where evident. The feelings of all were wrought up to the most fearful in enmity, nor was it until after the expiration of an hour that the thickly falling matter having expended itself over the soil left the polluted atmosphere once more open to the sun's regenerating and enlivening rays.—Never was the light of Heaven more rapturously hailed than at this moment, and the laboring and oppressed bosoms of thousands, trembling at the awfulness of their situation, were once more free to respire with freedom, and that with sentiments of gratitude to an Almighty Being for the preservation of those lives which few perhaps could have rendered up at that moment with hope and confidence. All was soon forgotten—again did the little suppressed sounds of busy industry make themselves heard—again did the planter riot in his sensibility—again did the ruffian manager brandish his lacerating slave whip, and again did the helpless African drag the chain which had been suspended only for an hour, and drop a tear at the reflection that he alone must be dead to all sensation of pity, and experience no participation in the delight which beamed on every other countenance. The lava, which had fallen about an inch in depth, proved to be an excellent manure, and from that hour the impoverished soil acquired all its original vigor. The influence of this phenomenon had been local and entirely confined to Barbados. A vessel approaching the Island to windward was the only exception, and her sails, yards and rigging were also literally covered with this dust. It is rather singular that some of the inhabitants should have thought of attributing the effect to its actual cause, but the darkness was so sudden that they had neither time nor power to reflect calmly on the subject and so fully impressed were they with the idea of the day being the last of nature that their astonishment on once more beholding the sun was little inferior to that they experienced at being so unexpectedly involved in utter and terrific darkness.

It is not uninteresting to behold how far nature has supplied in the sugar cane the various properties necessary for its transformation into that shape, which renders it so lucrative and valuable a commodity in commerce. In the first instance, the extreme scarcity of fuel in Barbados would render it no easy matter to boil the sugars, were the planters not indebted to the cane itself, after the syrup has been extracted—neither could any other description of wood produce the same volatile quick fire which is caused by this, and which according to managers, is indispensably necessary to the perfection of the sugar. In the next, where grass of any kind is so very scarce as to render it sometimes difficult to procure a sufficient quantity for horses alone, the working cattle would suffer materially—but here again the sugar cane is found to be of vital importance and remedies what would otherwise be a serious evil. The green tops or leaves which branch from it in shape not unlike those of the Indian corn, form the solid sustenance of the cattle, and this, although deemed too coarse a food for horses, is devoured by the former with avidity—and when great to these advantages the circumstances of thee crops being repeatedly removed without any further trouble being necessary than that of cutting them down and carrying them to the mills together with the additional extraction of molasses and rum from the same plant, it cannot be denied that the sugar cane is one of the most prolific as well as one of the most valuable productions of the earth.

Another singular plant, common to all the West India Islands, is the cassada root. This, when green, and immediately taken from the earth, is a rank and subtle poison, yet strange to say, it constitutes the chief article of food with the blacks, to whom it is given as a substitute for bread. To prepare it for this purpose the following process is used. While yet in its poisonous state, it is rasped by an instrument used for the purpose, and then spread over a dry floor, where it is suffered to remain unto the moisture, which contains the poison, is wholly extracted. When this fact is sufficiently ascertained, it is then considered fit for domestic purposes, and mixed with water, is made into large flat cakes scarcely thicker than a wafer. This bread is very much used and sold among themselves, and it is curious to behold with what dexterity a negro of either sex will carry a pile of these light cakes on their heads, seldom suffering one of them to fall, although from their constant wavering a stranger would fancy the whole about to tumble at every step taken by the carrier. These cakes are somewhat like the oaten, and if possible more insipid, yet do not contain much nourishment.

Another food but one which is considered quite too great a luxury for the slaves is the most disgusting animal to be found in any country—and that animal is the land crab. These filthy creatures, although well known to haunt the burial grounds, and to prey on human carcasses, constitute the chief delicacy of a West Indian table, and are eaten by the Planters whenever they can be procured. The mode of dressing them is by mincing very small, with copious use of spices and peppers, and then baking them in the shell in which they are served up. I have eaten frogs in France, notwithstanding every Anglophone prejudice, because I knew these animals to be perfectly clean, and that only the hind quarters are used for the purpose, but I never could conquer my repugnance so far as to meet the pressing solicitations of a West Indian host to taste a reptile that might lately have fed on some one of our companions and is ever loathsome and offensive to the sight.

No. 6.

A ludicrous circumstance connected with the land crab occurred while we were in Barbados. Not infrequently these reptiles may be seen marching in regular files from the sea to the hills and from the hills to the sea, as their necessities or cravings for food induce them. These marches are however performed at night so that they are generally secure, but not infrequently, on rising early for parade, they have been seen by the men using every possible speed in order to prevent their being surprised by the day, and often the heavy and less active stragglers have been found separated from their party and startled by the shrill notes of the bugle and the bustle of preparation redoubling their exertions at escape. This however they did not very frequently, under such circumstances, effect, the men seldom failing to evince their horror of them by their destruction. One night or rather one morning about two o'clock the Captain of the main guard, situated at one extremity of the parade ground, was startled from his imperfect slumbers by a succession of sounds similar to those produced by a body of dismounted cavalry with their heavy boot and spurs. His first impression was that the negroes had broken forth again into insurrection, but as the sounds drew nearer and appeared to enter from the pavement of the corridor or piazza into the guard room itself, he was instantly undeceived. The Subaltern on duty who had also availed himself of the Grand Rounds visit to compose himself to rest, and who lay extended on his guard bed at the opposite end of the room, was now awakened by his Captain, and as two heads are said to be better than one, they discovered by comparing notes and conjectures that the enemy who were still keeping up their infernal clatter, though in a more partial manner, could be no other than the land crabs. Their lamp had gone out, and there was no possible means of procuring a light. However as the noise gradually ceased they again laid down though little inclined to sleep, but they had not long resumed their original position when the blood of the Subaltern turned to ice in his veins on feeling several of these monsters crawling over his bed and limbs. Uttering an exclamation of horror he started to his feet, kicking one of the land crabs to the earth in the act. The Captain followed his example, and they both drew their swords, and commenced cutting in every direction on the paved floor, but their weapons only came in contact occasionally with the leg of a table or chair, overturning the one and wounding the other. The wary enemy were now tranquil, and the officers resolved to pass the remainder of the night in their chairs. But just as the Captain, overcome with fatigue, had fallen into a doze half sleeping half-waking, he felt one of his legs grasped by an enormous crab who began slowly to ascend his Hessian boot. He was a powerful man, and rising and shaking his captive leg with great violence, the enemy was soon thrown to the furthest extremity of the room. To hope for rest or quiet now was out of the question, and they continued to walk about until the day began to dawn, when the formidable column of assailants sallied out as they had arrived, and winding their way across the parade ground soon gained the more distant mountains. Had the guard been called out few of them would have escaped but as it was the officers either would not, or did not, think of summoning them for the purpose. When relieved on the following morning they were haggard from constant watching, and by no means inclined to desire a repetition of such a visit.

I recollect one night after having thrown myself down to rest in the same guard room, that my ears were some time assailed by a low sound as of scratching, which was discontinued at intervals. As I had no ambition to find myself in the vicinity of this bête d'antipatié—the land crab, I removed the clothes from the bed and closely examined the bedstead, but, finding nothing, replaced them and again lay down. I had not been long retired however when when the same sounds, though louder and evidently nearer my ear caused me to rise once more. Another examination succeeded but it proved equally fruitless, and after altering the position of the guard bed, I once more sought repose. The like sounds however still assailed my ears, and I was now resolved to leave no part unexamined. The clothes were again thrown off, and I turned the bedstead in every direction, when just beneath the head board I discovered a large crab with its glaring eyes fastened on the light held in my hand. It made no attempt to escape, but I would not have touched the monster on any consideration. I had therefore recourse to one of the black soldiers of a West Indian Regiment, several of whom had mounted the garrison guard with us, and he, delighted with the prize, caught it up between his fingers and carried it away to the main guard room where the enemy of my slumbers was soon killed, dressed, and eaten by the blacks of the guard.

The reptile which even the negroes hold most in terror and abhorrence is the wood slave. This little animal three inches in length seems to be of the lizard species, and generally of a dusty color, is rough and spotted like the toad, and most offensive to the eye. They are chiefly to be found in very old buildings where the wood is rotten, and affords an easy impression to their claws and feet, which are gradually worked in far beneath the surface. It would appear that these animals must subsist on air or on the rotten wood, for they will remain an inconceivable time wherever they chance to cling. To human flesh they will attach themselves in the same manner, and when they chance to fall on any part of the naked body, the instant application of a hot iron to their backs, is alone found successful in removing them. If suffered to continue even a short period the only means to be adopted is that of cutting out the flesh with the animal. The negroes have been frequent sufferers from these reptiles and can never look a them without dread and disgust.

Another great source of torment and annoyance to them is a description of reptile which they term a jigger. This animal is extremely minute and abounds much in the fresh waters which intersect various parts of the Island. It invariably fastens on the foot, and if not instantly perceived, works itself through the skin into the flesh where it deposits a kind of egg composed of numerous animalculae which are often fatal to the foot, not absolutely disabling, but rendering it ragged, misshapen, unhealthy, and hideous to behold. There are few blacks to be met with who, in consequence of going almost ever without covering to their feet, are not more or less afflicted with the malady produced by those tormenting jiggers. I once while bathing, got one of them in my heel, nor was I aware of the fact until a sharp and unusual pain in that part, some days subsequent, caused me to examine it. My black servant who was present looked at it also, and judging from the external appearance of the heel and the peculiar nature of the pain I described, instantly pronounced me to be in a "jiggery state." This intelligence alarmed me not a little, and already in imagination I beheld one foot swollen to twice the size of the other, but my attendant assuring me that he could remove without breaking it (for in this the danger lay) I submitted to an operation which he very dexterously performed with no other instrument than a needle, and to my great satisfaction, I soon beheld this formidable little intruder extracted, and happily for me in no way diminished in its bulk. They are much in size and appearance like a small maggot, or like one of those little white worms which may be seen on the leaves of trees in England after rain.

Many of the Islands of the West Indies abound in rats of an enormous size, but at Barados they are more common. These creatures frequently make the most desperate noises at night, and often convey the impression that a house is about to be broken open. In the latter Island there are a number of very small scattered wooden buildings in the vicinity of the Barracks, which are usually occupied by officers, and these houses tottering with a weight of years, are often shaken to their slight foundations by the galloping of rats along the walls and floors. They seem particularly partial to bedrooms, being possibly as luxurious as most other animals in the country, and very often take the liberty of insinuating themselves beneath the clothes. While inhabiting one of those old houses, I one evening, on going to bed, chanced to raise my pillow, when a huge rat sprang from beneath, and darting across the room, was soon lost in the surrounding gloom. I never ventured into bed again without cautiously examining my pillows and bed clothes, yet although I was not a second time honored with such a visit, I have passed many a sleepless night, in my horror of these animals, who often ran over my face and were only driven away by shoutings and the occasional traveling of my slippers and boots about the room.

No. 7.

Extreme laxity of morals has ever been considered peculiar to warm countries, but that refined voluptuousness which is at once the effect of education and climate in the southern parts of Europe is totally unlike what is practiced in the West Indies, where the gross sensuality, and the most inordinate indulgence, sink the unlettered and indolent Planter to the mere level of the brute. Reckless of consequences, unlike indifferent to public opinion, and to the effect likely to be produced on the minds of their female offspring by such conduct, they frequently, when tired of their society, and sated with possession, find pretexts for sending their wives to Europe, in order that they may indulge unrestrainedly in their illicit attachments to female, who are merely received for one moment, to give place to another the next. That no real or lasting affection should exist between married parties, in this country, cannot however excite surprise, since it can squarely be presumed that where there is no foundation established, in the cultivation of the mind, and in the observance of religious ordinances, there can be, much of that mutual esteem which is so indispensable to the harmony of matrimonial engagements. The very superficial requirements of the women have already been alluded to. Those of the men are, if possible, less and, with very few exceptions of a purely mercantile character; and the utter disregard evinced by both for the outward forms of worship, must not only tend to weaken a sense of the important nature of those ties by which they are indissolubly bound to each other, but to instill the pernicious poison of example into the minds of their children. The infidelities of the Fathers, even while living with their families, are seldom kept concealed from their daughters, and such example, acting on lively imaginations, must gradually weaken the horror of vice and prepare the mind for the reception of the same voluptuous expressions. This deplorable evil, for such it must be admitted to be, is less attributable to climate—although climate has, of course, its influence in producing it—than to the absence of proper education. Moreover in the West Indies there appear to be few persons who deem it all necessary to instill, either by precept or example, the seeds of religion into the minds of the children, and in this they are especially culpable; for, although the picture of licentiousness, which is hourly unfolded to her view, may act with fatal effect upon her mind and soften down the asperity of her disgust, there is no woman in whose breast the pure tenets of Religion and Morality have been made to take early root, who will not find strength to resist the influence of example, and pause long and deeply, before she finally decides on passing the barrier which leads to guilty indulgence.

If such be the state of moral and religious feeling amongst the whites, it will be difficult to understand that, with the people of color even a greater disregard of appearance is every where evident. Few marriages of any description are ever contracted, and the blacks live almost wholly in a state of nature, to which the frequency of temporary engagements, entered into between the whites and mulattoes, first reconciles and disposed them. A woman of color shows no shame whatever in submitting herself to the embraces of a man to whom she is connected by no tie of religion; and natural children are by no means regarded with that contempt to which they are so unfeelingly subjected in Europe. It is but justice to these women however to add, that the voluntary engagements into which they enter are, in many instances, held as sacred as if they were actually performed with all the imposing ceremonies of the church and where anything like real attachment has been felt, in the commencement of their intercourse, that feeling never wholly subsides, but rather increases as the ties of offspring awaken the more tender and affectionate feelings of the mother. Infidelity with these, is by no means a common failing, and when we consider that this portion of the society is wholly without the advantage of education, it must be admitted that they rank much higher in the scale of morality than the whites, for not having been taught to consider concubinage as a glaring vice, and fulfilling, to the extent they conceive necessary, the various duties imposed on them as mothers, and as partners of those with whom they cohabit, their discharge of the moral obligation may be considered infinitely superior.

As for the wretched blacks, sunk the lowest in this endless scale of color and degree, they are suffered to live even as the brutes of the field, and scarcely possess a sentiment beyond that of promiscuous intercourse. Nor is this at all to be wondered at since the planter alive ever to his own interest, even at the expense and sacrifice of every better feeling, instead of repressing the profligacy likely to arise between the sexes, thrown together by the various duties of their labors, rather encourages an intercourse, which, in affording the prospect of offspring, seems the most likely means of feeding his wealth. With this view are dances at the termination of their labors frequently countenanced among the younger negroes. It is by no means uncommon for an unmarried planter or manager to have several mistresses at the same moment, and as these women reside on the same estate, and are each aware of the affinity in which the others stand to their master, a thousand jealousies of course are the result. Should the proprietor or manager perceive and select any young female among his slaves, whose ripening beauty serves to inflame and act upon his depraved imagination, there is no obstacle thrown in his way, since from herself alone opposition can arise, and that she is never disposed to put in force, not only because she is not taught to consider incontinence a vice but because she fears to irritate her tyrant, and to provoke punishment by resistance. I have several times been present at parties given to single men only and after having partaken copiously of exhilarating wines, been introduced into the hall where the best looking of the young female slaves, with a few young men, have been assembled dancing to the discordant sounds produced by some old negro performer. Here the host, willing to extend the rites of hospitality to the utmost, has usually inquired of his guest whether any particular female pleased his eye, and if answered in the affirmative, soon made signal to the girl, which being understood, was instantly obeyed. Many of these young creatures did not exceed 12 or 14 years of age. The immorality thus encouraged by these men who ought, in some measure, to be held responsible for the conduct of their slaves, is glaring in the extreme, but what must excite the deepest astonishment and disgust in the breast of the European, is the fact of their suffering their own children, by these young negresses, to be classed among their slaves, and to serve and toil for them as such. And while it is the interest of the West Indian planter to keep the black population in that disgusting state of brutal ignorance, which alone tolerates these abuses, every attempt at the manumission of these unhappy creatures will not fail to meet with the most decided and vindictive opposition. Brutalized by oppression, and thrown out of the scale of human beings by the unceasing humiliations of their dependency, no wonder is it that the miserable negro often presents that character of imbecility, and a stubborn sullenness, on which tyrants found their chief arguments against emancipation. But what can be expected of men whose minds are necessarily debased by the most abject of all servitude. What but imbecility and obtuseness of character can be the result of a position, where, without sympathy between themselves and their oppressors, they are compelled to drag the yoke of never ending bondage, without and hope of reward for all their toil and sufferings, than the very faint and distant one of emancipation in their later years, when labor and punishment have worn them to decrepitude, yet ever with the cruel and lacerating slave whip suspended, like the sword of Damocles, eternally over their heads, and threaten at every instant to fall on these devoted victims to tyranny and caprice. That the negro is capable of appreciating and enjoying liberty is a fact that no one who has resided in the West Indies for any time, however short, can have failed to remark, therefore any argument to the contrary must be absurd. Ask a black who has, by some peculiar and fortuitous circumstance, obtained that liberty for which he has long respired, what are his sensations? They will inevitably be found to be those of profound joy and exultation. He feels himself a new being, and not only breathes with greater freedom, but like his erect person, when the lash has not wholly deprived it of the power of becoming erect, and his full eye, which, during servitude, is ever bent on the ground while in the act of addressing any one, glances with manly boldness on surrounding objects. Address such an individual under the impression of his being a slave, and he fires immediately. Inquire who is his master, and he replies, proudly and indignantly, that he is his own master, or he acknowledges no other than "King George." Liberty is unquestionably the first of human blessings, and, among his wretched and persecuted race, it is so highly prized as nearly to intoxicate them when obtained. Does this then argue inaptitude to appreciate the delights and advantages of freedom? To judge of his negro character, and even of their intellect, we must not take them in a state of cruel slavery, where the spirit is broken by the frequent application of the lash, and where the energies of the mind are blunted by unceasing toil. Could they look forward to the termination of their sufferings, at a given period of years, and consider their liberty as being then assured, they would appear (eve as slaves) in a very different light, but where no hope is held forth to future enjoyment—no term affixed to the servitude beneath which they groan, what but inertness, dulness, stupidity, and despair can they be expected to exhibit.

It is contended, by the enemies of emancipation, that, independently of their unfitness to enjoy liberty, if accorded them, the slaves are much better off, and possess greater advantages, in their neutral state, than they possibly could expect as freemen. If to be indifferently fed and clothed—to have but those hours to devote to the comfort of their families, and the cultivation of their little crops which are usually set apart for relaxation among the working classes in Europe—to have their health impaired by never ending toil and suffering—to have their bodies deformed and destroyed by cruel ruptures, many of them of singular magnitude and produced in great measure by hard labor—if to have their bodies hourly scourged by the lash of the task master, and to hear the appalling shrieks of their helpmates and children writhing beneath the same torture, if all these; and many more, are the advantages they derive from slavery; then may it be imagined that they would experience more happiness in a different condition, and find, in a handful of maize and a girdle round their loins, all that their absolute necessities require, while a consciousness of liberty would give vigor to their exertions, and enable them soon to derive benefits and advantages even greater than those which we are modestly told are attached to a state of slavery.

If the negro appeared to be deficient in intellect, he is very little worse than the being who is appointed to preside over his destiny, for with very few exceptions indeed, it would be difficult to find an equal number of men more brutal, more unlettered, or more ignorant of all things unconnected with the management of a slave plantation, than the Managers of Estates of the West Indies. Nor is this surprising, for it is a fact well known, that many of these people are actually thought as task masters, and that they frequently arrive in gangs, on a speculation of the kind, and are usually knocked down to the highest bidder. In this degrading manner is their condition, of slave-drivers, from whence they are, almost invariably, promoted to Managers, originally contracted for.

No. 8

Instances of cruelty are not wanting even with the better class of proprietors, yet it must be admitted, the evil principally lies with the delegates who abusing the unlimited authority invested in them during the absence of their masters, distort the letter of their instructions in their own views and caprices. That these are many highly respectable and humane proprietors to be met with, those who have resided for any time in the West Indies, can fully bear testimony—but that very respectability of education, and humanity of feeling, in rendering them more immediately sensible of the unfitness of the mass, to become their associates or friends, drives them frequently to the mother country, in search of kindred natures and nobler pursuits, and hence arise the misery of the slave. In no condition of life, can the operation of change be more keenly felt than in that of slavery, where the great portion of existence is suffering, and the occasional glimmering of comforts and pleasure (ever appreciated) are entirely comparative. Were it required, that the persons chosen to succeed them in these little governments, should be men of education and tried humanity, not only would the condition of the unfortunate black be greatly ameliorated; but it might be presumed the proprietor himself would feel a deep satisfaction arising from the conviction, that hundreds of human beings formed like himself, endowed with the same passions, and looking up to him for protection, while they toiled alone for his interest, were left in a situation no less secure, and under a guardianship no less humane than they had experienced with himself. But while the practice is continued of employing ignorant man, whose very abjection of nature, elicited in their ardor to obtain so disgusting a situation as that of a hireling manager, is in itself, a pledge of the natural cruelty of their dispositions, there can be no prospect of comfort for the slave.

That cruelty is almost ever the result of hardened and depraved vice, is a maxim that may find its confirmation in the difference of feeling and action, which distinguishes the West Indies endowed with moral principle, from him, who wallowing in brutal sensuality, serves no God but his own passions and acknowledges no power but his own will. Wherever a West Indian proprietor, by birth, education, and feeling a gentleman, is found surrounded by domestic ties, and cherishing the woman whom he has chosen as his companion through life—in short fulfilling in his own family, the various moral duties required by religion at his hands, the condition of the slave is even such as to convey a strong impression of his humanity; while on the contrary, with those who hold moral and religious observances in neglect, if not in absolute contempt, and gloat their swinish appetites in licentiousness, the most decidedly opposite effect is produced and offered to observation.

Amid the various feelings which swell highly in the breast of the European stranger, at the melancholy picture of human tyranny on one hand, and human suffering on the other, thus unfolded to his view, there is none more painful or more calculated to inspire unqualified disgust than that arising from a knowledge of the treatment of the slave by the free people of color. That the white who owns no affinity to, and even endeavors to persuade himself as a specious justification of his conduct that he is of a different nature from the black. That he should treat this oppressed race with cruelty, may though with difficulty be understood, but that those who are sprung from the same loins should prostitute the freedom, they, by mere accident enjoy, by rendering it accessory to the infliction of additional pain, and a prolongation and extension of the miseries of slavery, attached to their own race, is a fact which must excite the utmost horror and astonishment. If the white manager is cruel and exacting, the mulatto proprietor is not less so, and so far from seeing to soften down the hardships and humiliations attendant on the situation of the wretch, who toils and dies in the service of his own offspring, exercises all in his power with ever more unrelenting severity. Here is a picture which nature and humanity must shoulder, yet is it not surcharged. Is cruelty then inseparable from power, and are the cravings after wealth and authority such as to stifle the sentiments of nature within our bosoms! Painful as it is to admit the fact, it cannot well be denied, and ignorance and brutality must ever complete what selfishness and avarice have suggested and begun. Nearly as illiterate as the slave over whom they tyrannize, these people of color are with very few exceptions contracted in their ideas, vicious in their habits, unfeeling in their natures, insatiable in their avarice and groveling in their pursuits. Removed by their birth from that complexion which is the symbol of slavery, they still feel that the remove in the link of connexion is not sufficiently distant and appear as if desirous to visit the shame they secretly experience at being compelled to trace their origin to such a source on those who are the innocent cause.

When are the sufferings of these wretched people to find a term? and when will the Legislative authority of his country interpose between the tyrant and his victim?

At the close of a discussion in Parliament on the subject of a Petition from the free people of color during the administration of Mr. Canning to be admitted to the enjoyment of certain privileges which are now exclusively confined to the whites, that eminent Statesman made the following remark: "It was one thing to combat prejudice, nature, and an order of things that could not be countenanced, and another to plant human institutions for the purpose of correcting human evil and producing human good. The first was the resource of the Legislation, the last the province of manners; and the error arose from not observing the due limits of both, from not marking the difference between grievances which the Legislature could remedy and those which must be left to a slower process. He concurred with the honorable Member for Winchelsea that it was impossible justice should be done unless the prejudices of the Colonists were not broken down, but acted upon; first trying the power and willingness of the local Legislature, and interposing with the higher power of Parliament if it were found necessary. The whites, in one Island Jamaica, had been stated at 25,000; the blacks at 360,000; and there were besides 30,000 neutrals, whom the governing part of the community might win to themselves by indulgence and conciliation, and whom it would be absolute madness and the most incredible folly, with their eyes open, not to conciliate, and thereby gain a most important acquisition. He would leave the Colonists the means of obtaining this object as fast as they could by a conquest of prejudice, but he would exact from them a removal of the evil. If they did not remove it themselves it must be removed for them." Although these observations relate chiefly to the position of the free people of color, who are certainly most cruelly shut out from the many privileges, the latter sentence may be considered as applicable in an equal degree to the slaves, but if Mr Canning, at that period, looked forward to the eradication of prejudice in the minds of men so every way interested in the continuance of the present system, he certainly deceived himself, and that of course which he gave his pledge eventually to adopt if necessary must firmly be resorted to by some future minister; for no act of the Colonial Legislature of these Islands will ever be passed to meet the intention proposed. Prejudice must exist as long as self interest constitutes the ruling passion of the white population, and as little disposition will be evinced to admit the free people of color to a participation of those privileges, as to accord that to the blacks, which is not withheld from the vilest insect in the creation. Mr Wilmot Horton in the course of the same debate observed that "in his view, it was far wiser to wait until gradual improvement in education and property among the negroes had produced its influence on the Colonial Legislatures than to call upon those bodies peremptorily to change their system at once." In using the term "Negroes," the statesman possibly meant it to apply to the free people of color, for improvement in education and property among the slave population, must be as hopeless a prospect as that of tolerance and humanity among whites—and even among its free people of color, improvement of education must be viewed in comparative light, and as distinguishing them from the blacks, more by the state of barbarous ignorance, in which the latter are kept, than by any indication of more than common intellect among themselves.

Yet it cannot be denied, that however deeply humanity may deplore the existence of such glaring and desolating evil, and however warmly an enlightened ministry may enter into, and feel desirous of redressing such multiplied grievances, the act of absolute and compulsory emancipation would be delicate indeed. With no common prejudices to contend against; no economic obstacles to surmount; they must be prepared, not only to meet the passionate invectives of a body of passionate men, but to find a host of rebellious spirits arrayed in hostile opposition to the execution of their will. But if slavery must continue—if fate has so damned the unfortunate black, as to fetter him through succeeding ages with chains and bondage, may not certain acts of the Legislature at home be framed in amelioration of his condition? It has ever appeared to me feasible to blend the interests of humanity with those of the planter, by introducing some law in regard to the slaves which would necessarily strike at the root of those evils which are now the result of unlimited power, and irresponsibility of action. For instance an act might be passed to enfranchise every negro after reaching a certain age; let that of the male slave be 45, that of the female 40. The planter would then have the advantage of the services of each generation, and finding it to be his interest, to avail himself to the utmost of the term prescribed, would seek to conciliate the negro by good treatment; while the slave on the other hand, roused from that state of torpor which the anticipation of never ending servitude has thrown over his whole being, would become, as it were, regenerated, and seek to win the appropriation of his master, whose good offices and assistance might be necessary to him in the hour of emancipation. The number of actual slaves would of course be thus diminished, but here would be an additional motive for good treatment, for no longer compelled to toil as bondsmen to his service, the planter would find these people in no way disinclined to engage themselves as hirelings; and attached as well to gratitude as by habit and the ties of kindred to the estate, would require little more than what was originally accorded to them as slaves. Such a measure as this, I should conceive, might be successfully adopted, and would prepare the West Indians, by imperceptible gradations, and the practice of engaging hirelings, for the reception of the important question of absolute power and eventual emancipation. If it is to be left to time to operate a change of feeling on the subject with the proprietors, and it is palpable, that the moment of that operation is far distant, surely the sufferings and injuries of the slaves should not be wholly disregarded, and if tyranny and oppression will not bow to the suppliant voice of humanity, the arm of judicial authority should be raised in support of its appeal.

No. 9

In the summer of 1817, a general Court Martial being ordered to assemble in the Island of Grenada, for the purpose of trying several men of the York Rangers for desertion; one field officer, two captains, and several subalterns, were embarked for that destination the army gun-vessel Duke of York, kept for the purpose of transporting officers and conveying despatches from one Island to another. The field officer selected for this duty, was the Major of our Regiment, who had recently arrived from England to relieve the Colonel, then returning on leave, and to assume the command. On the after noon of the second day we came in sight of Grenada, whose lofty hills contrasted in no ordinary manner with the low country we had just quitted and as the more minute features of the Island developed themselves to our view, the eye hung with admiration on various points in the perspective. Rich and flourishing vallies clothed in green and teeming with the various produce of the climate, were everywhere visible between the dark and frowning masses, hose summit lay buried in the dense clouds perpetually rolling along these ridges of mountain, while, in the foreground, the town of St.

George, built on a sloping ground, rose like an ampitheatre before us, and created by the distant and imposing fortifications of Richmond Hill which, in the direction by which we approached, seemed to rise immediately over it, presented at once a picture of the beautiful and sublime. In a few hours we reached the commodious and landlocked harbour of the Carenage, and being speedily disembarked, were conducted by the Fort Adjutant to quarters assigned us in an old dilapidated Barrack , were the General Court Martial was to sit.

The town of St Georges is built much more in the English style than that of Bridgetown. The houses are in general good—chiefly of a lead color—and covered with red tiles, which gives them a pleasing appearance, and is far less offensive and injurious to the eye. The streets however are truly infamous, being paved with small rough stones which are exceedingly painful to the feet. Foot paths are luxuries unknown here, consequently men and beasts mix promiscuously in the middle of the streets, the stronger animal selecting the best part at the expense of the weaker. Immediately at the top of the town, and distinctly and pleasingly seen on approaching from the sea, are the Church and Parsonage, the latter half concealed amid a cluster of trees of rich foliage and ornamented with a lawn tastefully disposed. Viewed collectively and from a distance, the houses appear to wear an appearance of elegance, but when examined separately and minutely, not one habitation in the town of St Georges will be found worthy the attention of the stranger. The only building on which any taste or architectural skill appear to have been bestowed, is the Government House, situated about half way between the town and Richmond Hill Barracks, which are at the distance of a mile.—This building is capacious, and adapted to the purpose for which it was designed. It has rather extensive grounds attached to it, and is usually occupied by a General officer, who unites in his person the offices of Military Commander and Civil Governor. In Barbados many little villas are seen rising immediately on the skirts of Bridgetown. On an elevated and slightly projecting neck of land, the town of St. Georges is protected on one side, and the harbour on the other, by a strong fortification which commands the approach. This has however been much neglected, and the small barracks attached to it and fixed on for our temporary residence, seemed ready to tumble about our ears at every gust of wind.

The criminals summoned before the Court were six in number and all found guilty of repeated desertions. Three were condemned to die, and three to receive eight hundred lashes and have the letter D marked on their backs. The sentence of one of the latter was commuted from death to corporal punishment (although a very hardened character) on account of his age and the circumstances of his having two sons serving in the 71st Regiment. Here I cannot forbear remarking in the impropriety of suffering very young officers to sit on Courts Martial in cases of life and death; for, however disposed a young man may be to exercise his own judgment, there cannot be a doubt that it is often influenced by the opinions of his seniors in rank and years, and that even when he inclines to mercy, he delivers a contrary decision less in accordance with his own sense of the propriety of that decision, than with the necessity he conceives existing of adopting the maturer judgment of his superiors. Hence it not infrequently results that one or two voices, if not delivered in levity, at least in doubt, decide the fate of the unhappy criminal, and launch him with all his crimes upon his head into eternity. It is true that the sentence may be strictly just, but it is no less culpable in a member of so serious and imposing a tribunal, to pronounce his opinion, without having duly weighed and deeply considered every circumstance of the case, and where the life of a fellow being is at stake, it would be much better, in the event of doubt, to lean to the side of mercy, than to adopt the severer decisions of others. No officer who has not completed seven years of actual service, and attended at least as many General Court Martial as an attentive witness of the proceedings, should ever by selected for this purpose, and even then the President of the Court should be required not only to receive their simple opinions but to inquire of the junior Members on what particular points of the evidence adduced these opinions are principally grounded.

I make these observations because on this General Court Martial the first I had ever attended, I do not think my own experience was sufficient, and I greatly fear that in pronouncing sentence on these unhappy men, I was less governed by my own judgment than by that of the senior officers, who pointed out the nature of the crime and the penalty affixed to it by the articles of War. I know not whether the unwillingness I inwardly felt to adopt this severer decision was the result of the important character in which I stood, and of the awe and unpleasantness one must naturally entertain to deprive a human of existence, even in conformity with the laws of justice: but often since that period has the recollection of those unhappy men occurred to me, and as often have I wished that my voice, although it would not have turned the scale, had not been for death. Other members of the Court, even younger than myself, were, I have no doubt, influenced, in the same manner, for their experience was even less, nor were their judgments more mature. The only circumstance which can at all excuse the practice of summoning young and inexperienced officers to sit on General Courts Martial, is the difficulty of procuring a sufficient number to be spared from their regiments, who are better qualified for the duty. Yet in cases of so much importance to the criminal, it would seem not only more humane but more judicious to send the older and more experienced for this temporary purpose, and leave the discharge of regimental duties to the young officers. It is in the West Indies chiefly, that this practice, which time and reflection have taught me to deprecate, is suffered to prevail. In the present instance however it had been deemed necessary to have recourse to severe and summary measures in order to put a stop to desertion, which had become very frequent in the York Rangers. These troops were all what are termed condemned men, destined to serve in the West Indies for life, and, without any other chance of ever visiting their native shores than that afforded by desertion; and one of the criminals now sentenced to die, had been convicted of repeated offences. Even after he was reconducted to prison at the termination of his trial, he declared to the serjeant of the guard, that if he escaped with his life on the present occasion he would desert immediately afterwards. Mistaken man! he little imagined that at that moment a sentence was passing which would for ever arrest his future attempt, and that in a few days he would be summoned to expiate his numerous offences with his blood.

One of the greatest annoyances to every regiment going to the West Indies, is that of having numbers of these condemned men drafted into them from those they relieve. Doomed to serve in this climate alone they are handed over to each corps in succession, and mixing with the mass of the regiment often corrupt by their example men of hitherto irreproachable character. Conscious that the clime in which they serve must receive their bones, they become at once reckless of life and indifferent to punishment. Shame that has long ceased to operate on the minds of men habituated to, and enduring the penance of crime, fails to inspire that natural horror of humiliating punishment, which tends indirectly to the production of good, and they are, in consequence rendered obdurate and intractable.—Three hundred of these men were sent to us on the arrival of the Regiment in the West Indies, and proved a source of perpetual anxiety to their officers. In the company to which I was attached were three or four of these fellows, who seemed far to surpass their companions in sloth and filthiness, and attention, and these men gave me more trouble than all the rest of the company together. One in particular must, I am persuaded, have been flogged a dozen times in six months, for no sooner was he out of hospital than he was brought to the triangles again. This man was incorrigible. He used to bear his punishment with sullen and uncomplaining endurance, and I am convinced that when finished he used to congratulate himself on the prospect of continuing a few weeks longer in hospital, and thereby evading the trouble and fatigue he appeared to find in the discharge of his duty.

No. 10

The object of our visit to Grenada being accomplished, we again embarked in the Duke of York for Barbados, but it was destined that all should not return with life. Our Major had complained on the morning of embarkation for the first time of head ache which increased in violence every hour, and ere the sun had set behind the horizon, he was in a state of absolute delirium. The excitation produced by close application in his capacity of President of the Court, and by exposure to the night air in returning from distant parties, where more wine was usually drank than would be prudently done by one recently arrived from Europe, tended to produce fever. With but a few and very indifferent medicines on board, and no one to administer them with skill, his situation was almost hopeless, but we made so much progress during the day, as to induce a belief that we should reach the Island of Tobago in time to save his life. Here we did not however land him until the following day, and then he was in a state of extreme exhaustion. We were hospitably received by a gentleman residing on that part of the Island at which we touched, and a bed was instantly prepared for the reception of the patient. The moment a medical man could be procured the usual remedies were applied, and the Major found himself relieved. Anxious to return to his Regiment and his duty he insisted on being reconducted to the vessel, when notwithstanding every remonstrance to the contrary we again set sail and continued our course for Barbados. The same evening he grew worse and fainter, taking no other nourishment than a little tamarind water, and eventually again delirious. His ravings were loud and painful, and all his thoughts seemed to linger on battalions and divisions, which he fancied he was putting through their evolutions. At length he grew calmer though his respiration was thick and heavy, and at three in the morning he died. Thus perished in the vigor of manhood an officer for whose character even during the short period he had been with us, the whole Regiment had conceived the highest esteem. Strict but not harsh, exacting the fulfillment of duty to the letter, but not rendering that duty unpleasant by frivolous and vexatious animadversions—studying the comforts of the men—making allowances for, while he reproved the faults of the young officers, a stern commander in the field but a perfect gentleman at the mess table, he was considered by the corps, in the light of one whom a more intimate acquaintance with it would have rendered at once a Father and a friend.

Although we knew decomposition to succeed death in the course of a few hours, we were resolved to carry the body to Barbados with us, and an arm chest was procured for the purpose of receiving it. Covered with the Union flag of the vessel it was then placed on deck, but the effluvia soon became highly offensive, and had at the expiration of twenty-four hours, increased to such a pitch that the sailors began to murmur and intimate the necessity of the body being thrown into the sea to prevent contagion. We however prevailed on them to wait a little longer, promising to do so, if we did not make land within a certain time. The wind was fair and we were rapidly advancing towards our destination, so that we hoped to be spared this alternative, nor were we wrong, for the low hills of Barbados soon afterwards appeared before us, and in a few hours we reached Carlisle bay where the body was instantly landed and prepared for internment. Preceded by the full and sonorous band playing the Dead March in Saul to which the mournful trappings of his led horse, bearing his boots ornamented with the field officers spurs, lent additional interest, and followed by the officers of the Garrison, the remains of our late Commander were conveyed to the burial ground in Bridgetown where finally they were deposited. This was the only instance I ever witnessed of a funeral being conducted with military honors in Barbados, and I believe there were few officers of our corps who could have patiently brooked its absence on the present occasion.

We found on our return to Head Quarters that a change of Garrisons was meditated and the wings of our Regiment was as we had long anticipated, about to be divided and sent to different destinations. This was by no means unpleasant intelligence inasmuch as it related to our removal from an Island where eternal drills and parades were the order of the day, but the inconvenience and annoyance of what we knew would be a separation of years among ourselves, we felt to be great. A troop ship conveying the Regiment which had been for several years divided in this manner, and was now destined to relieve us preparatory to its return to Europe soon afterwards arrived, when our right Wing embarked under the senior surviving Captain for St. Vincents. The intermediate time was employed by ourselves in procuring whatever was necessary for our mess table. Everything—glass, plate, linen, and cutlery having been conveyed to Head Quarters; and here is an additional expense to which these, whose lot it is to be attached to the left Wing of a Regiment are ever liable on leaving the Barbados. On the return of the ship from St. Vincents we were immediately embarked, and wafted by a gentle and favorable breeze, soon came in sight of our destination, which was the Island I had so recently quitted. Once more did the lofty hills of Grenada unfold themselves in sombre Majesty to my admiring view, and again did I behold with pleasure the vallies, the town, and the parsonage. Boats were in readiness for disembarkation, and in an hour from the moment of our casting anchor—the troops were all landed and on their march for Richmond Hill Barracks.

The first duty we were called to perform on our arrival was the melancholy one of carrying into effect the sentence of the court martial —the execution of which had been prudently deferred until the arrival of another corps. Accordingly one morning, the whole of the garrison appeared under arms, drawn up in a low ground immediately beneath the barracks, which was used as a parade. The troops consisting of a few artillery, the York Rangers, and our Regiment, occupied three sides of a square, and on the fourth were placed three coffins at equal distances from each other. A clergyman in his robes of office was present, ad the most impressive silence pervaded every rank. One settled look of serious melancholy was discernible in the features of both officers and men, and the words of command were even given in a lower tone of voice. Every individual seemed to find his situation painful, and the minutes which intervened until the arrival of the condemned were passed in anxiety and awe. It had been feared that an attempt at rescue would be made by their comrades and our corps had in consequence been secretly ordered to provide themselves with ammunition while care was taken by their own officers, that the Rangers should have none. At length the unfortunate men appeared slowly advancing surrounded by their guard, and as they entered the open space in front of the troops, I saw one of them point me out to one of his companions, as he addressed some observation to him. I could not hear what he said, but presumed, that as I was the only officer attached to this division of my regiment, who had been present at the trial, he was alluding to me as one of his judges. My feelings were much tried at this moment, and I would have given any thing to have been absent from this scene, but that was impossible. Soon afterwards, the criminals moved towards the line, prayed separately, and for a few minutes with the minister of religion. This being ended the clergyman withdrew, when the fatal caps were drawn over their faces, and they remained motionless, with their hands tied across and suspended in front. Three sections consisting of men drafted for the occasion, from their own corps, and commanded each by a corporal, were then silently drawn up in front of the coffins. No command was delivered, everything was done by signal, and as their pieces were directed against the hearts of their companions, that which was to launch them into eternity was given, and one simultaneous blaze of light flashed along the line of sections—not a groan was uttered—one fell dead on his coffin—another bounded several feet from his knees into the air and then sunk lifeless on his head—the third was the only one who suffered—the balls had not touched a vital part, and he lay writing in agony on the ground—two of the reserve immediately advanced with a corporal, and approached so near that a part of the poor wretches head was blown away, presenting a most cruel spectacle, and his struggles were at an end.

No. 11

This painful duty accomplished, the line was wheeled back into divisions and in conformity with the practice usual on such occasions, marched in slow time past the bodies and coffins of the criminals. Here however our task was not ended, for the sentence of the remaining prisoners was to be carried into execution, and a second party conducting the men who were to be flogged soon afterwards appeared. The triangles were soon prepared, and the furnace which was to heat the ignominy-stamping iron lay smoking at a distance. Being quickly stripped, the first who was to suffer extended his arms and legs for the purpose of being secured to the triangle, and beneath the eyes of his fellow criminals, who must have suffered nearly as much in the anticipation as in the actual punishment itself, received as many lashes of the number awarded as the medical men present pronounced him capable of enduring. The hot iron was then brought forward, and beneath its hissing surface, on a part of the back which remained untouched by the lash, was traced the character which to a soldier is ever that of infamy. The other prisoners were successively tied up, flogged, and branded, nor was it until a late hour in the morning that this scene terminated.

Of all the capital punishments inflicted by man on man, a military execution is at once the most imposing and the most affecting. The criminal who perishes on the scaffold is often a stranger to the thousands who, attracted by vulgar and unfeeling curiosity, rush tumultuously to witness the writings and sufferings of a fellow being. No feeling save that of instinct finds entrance in their bosoms, and even at the solemn moment of death the most disgusting scenes of contention frequently occur. Often does the coarse and brutal jest of some ruffian call forth the still more brutal laugh of the populace, and mingling with the last prayer of mortality, outrage both nature and humanity. The pangs of the victim are witnessed by the mass without emotion, and the spectacle is viewed only with the eagerness of curiosity which would be exhibited at a tragic representation on the stage. Few return better than they came, or benefit by the example they have witnessed, and when they relate the tale of ignominy and death to their children, it is less with a view to inculcate a salutary precept, than to impress them with a high opinion of their knowledge, or of the wonders they have seen. How different is the other. The soldier criminal, when conducted to suffer the penalty of his crimes, beholds in each individual a friend and a companion, and in the awful silence of that moment traces feelings even amid the gloom of inflexible features, which are only checked by a deep sense of military subordination. Men who have been nursed in camps, and hourly accustomed to the sight of blood, feel their hearts sink within them at the anticipation of the scene which is to follow, yet though their sympathies are deeply excited no murmur escapes their lips, for all acknowledge the justice of the sentence. No other image is suffered to engross their attention, but absorbed in contemplation of what is passing, they await in motionless attention the termination of the tragedy, and as the tearless eye of the veteran glances on his officer, he feels that such even would be his fate were he to violate those articles of military law which entail the penalty of death. The feelings of the officer are no less moved, but with him as with the soldier, they are only expressed in the stern fixedness of his gaze, and the gloom which overspreads his features. Nor is the solemnity of the last act of justice interrupted by any other sounds than the reports of the instruments of death, and the occasional groaning of the victims. All else is still and motionless as the grave, and when aroused from the statue-like appearance they have hitherto maintained, the numerous columns have been marched slowly past the bodies of the criminals, they return to their quarters with minds deeply impressed with solemnity and dread at what they have witnessed, and inclined to become better soldiers, and better men.

COMMENTARY

This essay appeared in the same volume II of Richardson's *New Era* newspaper as his *War of 1812.* He said it was taken from notes, which he made during his stay in the West Indies. He prepared the notes for publication for a liberal newspaper in England some time after the brief George Canning administration of 1827, from which he quoted comments from Canning, who was against slavery, and M. P. Wilmot-Horton and before the Emancipation Act of 1833. By his vivid descriptions of the terrible treatment of the slaves and the savageness of the West Indian society, Richardson eviscerated the stand taken by West Indian planters that their slaves were economically indispensable. The reader senses that he, as a military man, resents having to protect these planters from slave uprisings. His first duty is to guard the prison where slaves captured in the recent insurrection, almost certainly provoked by the planters for political reasons, lie incarcerated and the heads of many insurrectionists sit on poles in long rows.

In the first section he shows his anger at any break-down in discipline. An occasion for revelry, as a welcome relief from army rules, he condemns as if he were incapable of having boisterous fun. His humor was satirical. He did have empathy for his fellow humans, as he demonstrates in his descriptions of the punishment of the deserters and sympathy for the slaves, and this became more pronounced as he matured. He had an enquiring intellect and suggested a cause for the yellow fever and changes to the regimen of the army.

The diseases—in particular yellow fever which killed many but failed to kill him, probably because his system was prepared for it after his bout with the ague in Canada—are as threatening as the animals, especially the ugly land crabs. He thought that the fever came from the effluvia of swampy ground; it was not till the 1890s that Walter Reed and his colleagues discovered that the swamp mosquito carried it to humans. His most vivid descriptions, however, show the horror of military punishment—execution and lashing and branding—for desertion. The soldiers sent to the West Indies are there for life and will never see England again unless they can escape. The experience of watching the suffering of men, whom he judged in their Court Martial, haunts him. He transmutes that guilt to the reader. Years later when back in Canada, he suggested ways in which the desertions from British regiments in Canada to the United States could be prevented. By that time the lash had been banned as punishment, although as he saw during his service under Brigadier Evans in the British Auxiliary Legion in Spain, it was still used.

After two years the military life of drills of a peacetime army and the dullness of West Indian existence soon decided him to retire on half-pay back to England.

Pursuing journalism and literary work, his military life seemingly behind him, he, escaping an unhappy marriage in Paris, courted action in some distant field by volunteering at the war office at the London Horse Guards and seized an opportunity to join the British Auxiliary Legion in Spain. Although engaged in battle, he became disillusioned with the make-up of this mercenary army so different in spirit to the men he had fought alongside in the Napoleonic Wars. His strong individuality, evident in his West Indian recollections, communicated his dissatisfaction with the manner in which the Legion was led, more avoiding battle than engaging in it, and the diffidence of many of his fellow officers, thus making him enemies.

Later in Canada, he sold his half-pay status, thus losing his pension, to buy a press, from which he issued the *New Era*, in which he serialized his satiric novel about the Legion, "Jack Brag in Spain". The military took its revenge in little ways and his life became harder. In Montreal when editor of the *Montreal Courier* and after failing to make his own newspaper, the *Weekly Expositor,* successful, he lost faith in developing a more responsive culture to literature. The British-French riots over the Rebellion Losses Bill in 1849 dismayed him. As the parliament buildings were burning, he ran into the blaze to try to save as much of the library as possible.[7] To escape to where his talents could be appreciated and to publish his manuscripts, he went to the growing literary capital of New York City, where the masses were awakening to intellectual and artistic pursuits. In that cosmopolitan and idiosyncratic milieu, he sported the ribbon of the Spanish Military Order of San Fernando, given him for bravery, as a token of the institution he had once loved. Henceforth on the title-pages of his books, he inscribed KSF after his name.

[7] In *The Canadian Don Quixote* I mistakenly gave the credit to Stewart Derbishire, but the description of the unnamed rescuer fitted Richardson who had a large mustache whereas Derbishire had none and Richardson was indeed the editor of the *Montreal Courier*. [*Punch in Canada*, May 5, 1849]

IN SEARCH OF RICHARDSON'S SPAIN

In 1837, Major John Richardson, Canada's first and most colourful novelist, published in England *Movements of the British Legion*, a revision of his *Journal* published the previous year and critical of the Legion's commanding officer, George de Lacy Evans. Its reception was sensational because the Tories used it in Parliament to condemn the Whig government for sending British troops to help the Spanish Queen Maria Cristina subdue the rebelling Basques under the pretender Don Carlos. Scribbling in the minutes spared from his demanding work with the Commissariat of the Legion, Richardson described a unique historical experience—the long circuitous march in 1835 that eleven British regiments of over 40,000 men took through the Cantabrica Mountains from Bilbao south along the Atlantic coast then directly inland over the mountains to the plains south of Vitoria to rendez-vous with the Spanish army. Critical of the Lieutenant-General Evans for planning this evasive and costly maneuver, Richardson, nevertheless, praised it as, "one of the best conducted of any yet undertaken by men wearing the British uniform, and as such, deserves a page in future history." Fearing an ambush by Carlist guerrillas, several battalions of Chappelgorries or Red Hats—Basques, loyal to the Spanish government—led the way over the unfamiliar countryside. What took the Legion five weeks on foot, I could accomplish in a couple of days by car.

Passing through the large industrial city of Bilbao, I spent my first night in the Basque town of Lekeitio on the Atlantic coast, which, being the size of Bilbao in Richardson's day, would serve as a model of the city that introduced Richardson to Spanish ways. "The men are indolent to a proverb," Richardson wrote, "and spend their nights and days (those hours only which are devoted to meals excepted) in the cafes, where smoking, chattering (that is the word), cards, billiards, and dominoes, form their invariable and eternal pastime. As for the women, their only care, after marriage, seems to be to 'suckle fools and chronicle sour wine'." I noticed no greater fools than there are in other parts of the world, no suckling of them in public, and no sour wine, but I agreed with Richardson's observation on the male population, particularly with "chattering." From five in the afternoon to dinner at ten, the townspeople strolled along the quay, sat in the cafes, and stood at the windows of their homes "chattering." The sound reminded me of birds gathering in the hundreds in trees before sundown. Men broke into militant Basque songs. At dinnertime, the noise increased from the restaurants in the open air and continued until one in the morning.

Richardson, descrying the dominance of the Church, was pleased to see the people turning Churches into armories, although the black-robed priest, usually of sombre mien, was conspicuous. I rose before the hotel door was open and went to the quay. The town slumbered, save for a handful of fishermen loading a boat, a young man sketching the coastline, two girls and an old man with a cane wading in bare feet along the beach, and a priest who paced the quay, Bible in hand and deep in thought. The stone walls of the quay carried the black painted accusations of Basque militants: "Police—Assassins."

Driving along the banks of the Marbionne River, bringing sea traffic to Bilbao, I recalled Richardson's description: "commanding the most lovely view." Richardson would see today rows of workers' housing in grimy narrow streets, the cluttering of the river with freighters, heaps of slag and coal, factories, cranes, gas fires, billowing black smoke. Depressed by the contrast, I stopped to watch the citizens of Portugalete, swarming the streets to celebrate the anniversary of the Angel's announcement to Mary that she was to give birth, a small band marching and tootling, and a conveyance suspended by wires from steel beams carrying people across the river.

Richardson wrote: "It was truly a picturesque sight to behold the long line of troops, English and Spanish, as they wound, accompanied by a host of baggage mules and horses, along the banks of the river to Soroza...." Today the route runs on the sides of the gentle slopes of dark green hills interspersed with large drums of petroleum owned by Shell refining.

As I turned apprehensively inland to meet the national highway to Castro Urdiales on the Atlantic Ocean, the hills became higher, the valleys deeper, and the copses and woods more sylvan. Richardson described the fatigued soldier's wife with swollen feet marching bravely in pain, the frequent upsetting of baggage, and the squabbling muleteers. Banditti wounded two legionnaires, attacked an advance party of rifles, and kidnapped children lagging behind. Richardson, in the rear of the last brigade entering Castro, rode alone at sunset on a ridge of rock "that reverberated my horse's footfall in a most alarming manner, while my figure was thrown into bold relief against the sea that murmured in the distance, so that any one, hostilely disposed, might have picked me off from the dark rocks on my left, with perfect ease and without hazard."

Richardson found Castro Urdiales "a small, seaport town, remarkable only for the imposing appearance of its sea-girt, rock-based castle." The port is large now, stretching far along its beach. Below the ruins of the castle are the narrow streets of the old town. Castro's ancient air seemed to inhibit commercial projects from taking hold there as they have done in the next coastal town of Laredo, to which Richardson was sent by ship for intelligence reasons. From the ship, Richardson watched the troops, ascending the mountains toward Limpias, reach "the highest point of elevation, where their forms and glittering arms, thrown into bold relief against a cloudless sky formed a picture in itself as instinct with interest as with life." Impatient to leave these impersonal sea towns with their long stretches of silent apartment blocks, I drove inland to reach the heights.

The coastal and parallel inland roads, built in the tenth and eleventh centuries, were now B-roads, much improved over their state in 1835. The C-road connecting them, which I took, was paved but tortuous.

The forest closed tightly overhead on the winding drive through the mountains to Limpias. I could imagine the legionnaires' fears of ambush by Basque guerrillas. At Liendo, I encountered Mount Risco, at 4300 metres the highest mountain. High, sharply turning roads with magnificent views of small villages, trout streams and long sloping hillsides, this terrain on a sunny day was a delight by automobile. Richardson wrote: "...a district so mountainous that, perhaps, there is no instance on record of English troops having ever accomplished an equally arduous march."

The Legion rested a day at the village of Limpias. Its stream, flanked by fields of maize, ran by orchards crammed with luscious fruit and the spacious flower gardens of villas. General Evans had soldiers flogged for plundering the natives—the first breach of discipline.

I drove past highland farms and towns in the smaller hills and looked, quoting Richardson, "achingly down upon the pigmy world below" as I climbed "through one of these passes, bounded on the right by a precipice of many hundred feet of perpendicular descent, and on the left by a tall crag, nearly musket-shot in height, the bold yet regular sides of which assimilated it rather to some tower of strength, the work of human hands, than the sport of capricious Nature, who has scattered her grandeur over these remarkable provinces with so unsparing a hand. Fifty Carlists, placed upon the summit of that crag, might have annihilated the whole Legion...."

Clambering up the grassy knoll above the highway at the summit of Los Tornos, I happily found the cut of the old road through the cliff overgrown and forgotten. "Here, indeed, was a concentration of the sublime and beautiful," commented Richardson, who had taken an hour on horseback to ascend Los Tornos and surveyed far below the "alternate cornfield and pasture...like a carpet of many colours." The road plunged into a long valley, over Rio Carneja and through Agnera and Quintavella, flourishing with cattle and sheep, as Richardson described, before reaching Villesante, where the Legion camped that night. I visualized Richardson's journal entry for that day: "Two brigades are bivouacked in the open air, and their appearance is truly picturesque, the light of their cheerful fires casting that of a very brilliant full moon, completely into the shade. "

After Medina del Pomar, which Richardson described as "a rude old Moorish town," now an uninteresting combination of old and new buildings, I passed through a number of villages—Bastillo, Moneo, Pradolamatar, Nofuentes—poor and dry-looking. The hills, majestic and wild, began again at Tresperaderne. Crossing the small bridge over the River Ebro, I stopped to reflect at the "lonely" spot where Richardson pondered upon its association with many events in military history. Its solemnity awed him: "the hollow echo of [the river's] fall...was full of gloom, and came rather as the disturbed spirit of the wild...." It still captured that haunting, romantic aspect and brought me closer to understanding Richardson's soul, which, fashioned by the harsh realities of the Canadian wilderness, sought the refining interpretations of European thought.

Ona, a village in a rocky pass over the Ebro, remained vividly in my mind from my reading of the *Movements*. Here was the great monastery, "that might form a palace for an eastern emperor," whose vast, interminable cells, corridors and courts could accommodate the whole Legion, and whose subterranean passages recalled to mind "Mrs. Ratcliffe's well-known *Mysteries of Udolpho*." Richardson dined in its refectory, condemned the courses—"dried, insipid fish eaten with very bad oil"—but praised the quality of the bread. None of the monks appeared in the refectory, and the lay brethren served the legionnaires with indifferent good will. Richardson spent the night "on the naked floor of one of the principal rooms." Did it still exist?

Driving with great anticipation from the road along the river's edge into the village, which no longer fitted Richardson's description: "nowhere to be surpassed in meanness and poverty," I saw the monastery. It was now a huge hospital. I did not enter it; simply looking at its grandeur from the outside was sufficient. The chapel and sacristy joined it from the left side. "The former," wrote Richardson, "is of a gorgeousness commensurate with the vast extent and general richness of the whole building." That, indeed, was true. "The latter, handsomely decorated, is filled with scriptural subjects and portraits by the best masters." Probably still true as well. I peeked through iron bars set up to prevent the visitor from penetrating and noticed a priest escorting privileged visitors about the interior.

From the Ebro, narrow and aquamarine at this point, I climbed out of the pass into pretty hills through Pino de Bureba where the land became flat with many pine trees. Driving through Los Barrios at Rio Oca, I stopped at Aguilar de Bureba, a smelly, dirty village, where I photographed the twelfth century Romanesque Church ruin on the small hill overlooking the plain that Richardson would have seen. The country, commented Richardson, "was so level—not a mountain to be seen above the horizon in front—so unlike that to which we had latterly been accustomed, that we could scarcely persuade ourselves we were in the same region."

On reaching Brivieska, I understood that the fundamental character of a place never changes when I read Richardson's description: "one of the most wretched places under the sun.... The people are miserable... there is an apathy of manner about them, in the midst of all their filth and meanness, which provokes and vexes even more than their poverty." Unlike Richardson, who was obliged to spend three weeks there, I merely stopped to take a drink at the cafe (dirty) in the town's main square and confirm his verdict.

The high road leading to Vitoria—which Richardson declared "remarkably good, scarcely to be surpassed in any part of England"—cuts on the side of a mountain just above the rooftops of the village of Pancorbo, tunnels for a short distance through the rock and swoops down to the plain. Richardson slept at Pancorbo, "singular and romantic-looking...situated in the very heart of a pass, formed by immense masses of bold rock, literally overhanging the place." He took a side trip east on military business to Santo Domingo, where he saw "beautiful milk-white goats...browsing on the leaves of the brown-nut tree." I, however, followed the route of the Legion through the wide valley to Miranda de Ebro—with some regret as I wondered if the goats still existed.

Miranda's old town of narrow streets on the south bank is connected by a couple of bridges to the newer town on the north bank. Richardson remarked on the great confusion in Miranda as the masses of the Legion clogged the narrow streets for hours and waited to be quartered. I, in turn, from my hotel balcony, observed confusion in the hours before dinner when Spaniards, walking and talking, milled in crowds, and the cycles and autos streamed over the bridges and into the narrow streets on either side of the river.

The drive to Vitoria was short and straight. The old city of magnificent squares and long avenues had changed little from 1835, but, in the western section, modern boulevards, apartment blocks, hotels, and shops expanded it. When the Legion marched into the city behind its drummers and buglers, Richardson wrote: "A few 'vivas los Inglesas' burst from the crowd, but they were neither so universal nor so enthusiastic as we had been prepared to expect. Indeed, from what little I have been enabled to remark since our arrival, the inhabitants of Vitoria are infinitely more Carlists than Queenites." I saw no signs calling for an independent Basque state, but I pondered, like Richardson, on the secret sentiments of the citizens.

Vitoria was the Legion's nemesis. Typhus killed many of the troops under the most appalling conditions. Richardson almost died. From that point, his fortunes with the Legion declined. He fought in the battle of San Sebastian in 1836, but it is safe to say that the most remarkable experience of the legionnaires was this long, arduous, circuitous march from Bilbao to Vitoria. The motorcar made the journey enjoyable and allowed me to connect in spirit to the man whose sense for adventure and extraordinary creativity gave birth to Canadian literature.

—David Richard Beasley, Simcoe, ON

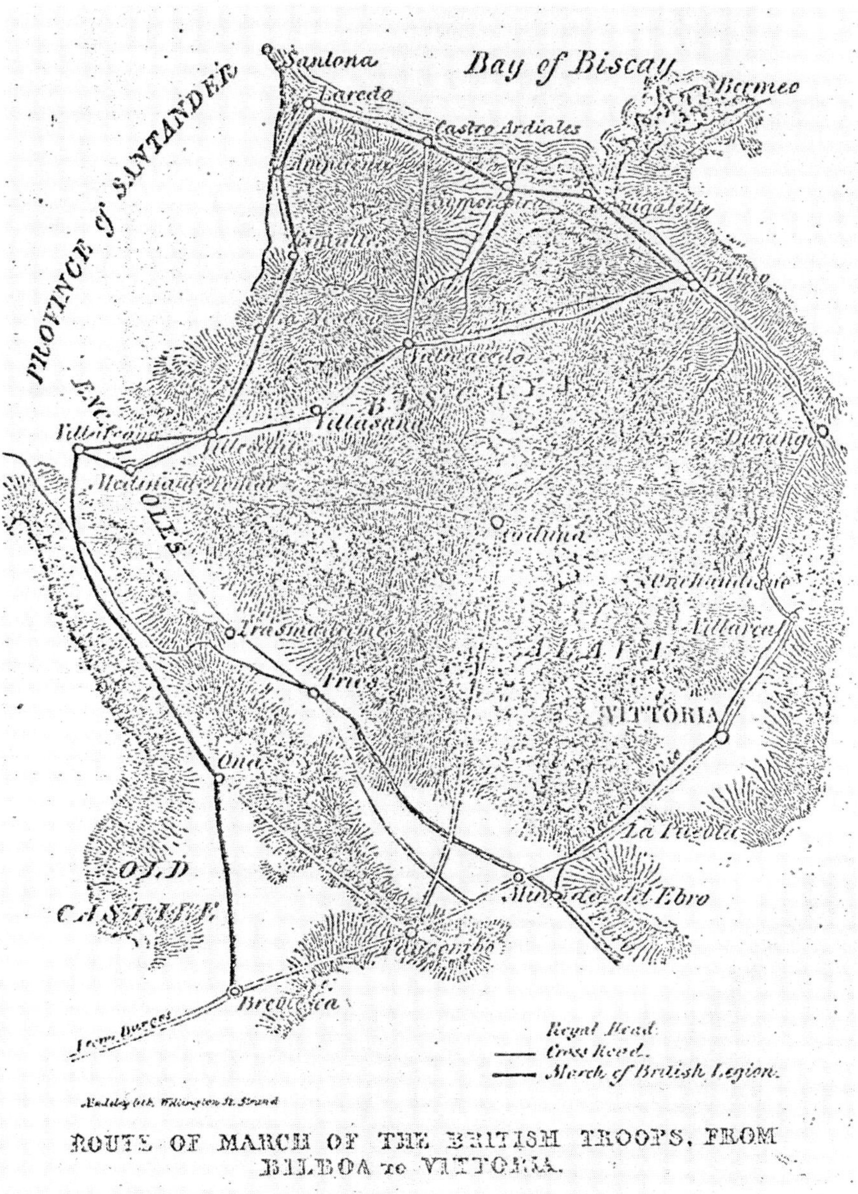

This map is taken from Richardson's *Journal of the Movements of the British Legion in Spain*. The march began in Bilbao, top right, along the thicker black line down the coast to Laredo, inland in a roundabout way to avoid the Carlists through Villesante, Ona, Brivieska and Miranda del Ebro to Vitoria where it joined the Cristinos army. [Vitoria is misspelled on the map].